Gra
Preface

ANTONY
AND CLEOPATRA

Foreword by
Richard Eyre

NICK HERN BOOKS

First published in this collected paperback edition in 1993 jointly by
Nick Hern Books Limited, 14 Larden Road, London W3 7ST
and the Royal National Theatre, London,
by arrangement with Batsford.

Preface to Antony and Cleopatra. Originally published in 1930

Set in 10/11 Baskerville by Pure Tech Corporation, Pondicherry
(India)
Printed in Australia by
Australian Print Group

A CIP catalogue record for this book is available from the British
Library

ISBN 1 85459 186 X

Shakespeare Alive!

The history of the theatre in England in this century can be told largely through the lives and work of two men: George Bernard Shaw and Harley Granville Barker, a triple-barrelled cadence of names that resonates like the ruffling of the pages of a large book in a silent public library. One was a brilliant polemicist who dealt with certainties and assertions and sometimes, but not often enough, breathed life into his sermons; the other a committed sceptic who started from the premise that the only thing certain about human behaviour was that nothing was certain. Both, however, possessed a passionate certainty about the importance of the theatre and the need to revise its form, its content, and the way that it was managed. Shaw was a playwright, critic and pamphleteer, Barker a playwright, director and actor.

The Voysey Inheritance is, at least in my opinion, Granville Barker's best play: a complex web of family relationships, a fervent but never unambiguous indictment of a world dominated by the mutually dependent obsessions of greed, class, and self-deception. It's also a virtuoso display of stagecraft: the writer showing that as director he can handle twelve speaking characters on stage at one time, and that as actor he can deal with the most ambitious and unexpected modulations of thought and feeling. The 'inheritance' of the Voyseys is a legacy of debt, bad faith, and bitter family dissension. Edward's father has, shortly before his death, revealed that he has been cheating the family firm of solicitors for many years, as his father had for many years before that. Towards the end of the play Edward Voysey, the youngest son, confronts the woman he loves:

> EDWARD. Why wouldn't he own the truth to me about himself?
>
> BEATRICE. Perhaps he took care not to know it. Would you have understood?
>
> EDWARD. Perhaps not. But I loved him.
>
> BEATRICE. That would silence a bench of judges.

Shaw would have used the story to moralise and polemicise. He might have had the son hate the father; he might have had him forgive him; he might have had him indict him as a paradigm of capitalism; he would never have said he loved him.

Everybody needs a father, or, failing that, a father-figure. He may be a teacher, a prophet, a boss, a priest perhaps, a political leader, a friend, or, sometimes, if you are very lucky, the real one. If you can't find a father you must invent him. In some ways, not altogether trivial, Granville Barker is something of a father-figure for me. He's a writer whom I admire more than any twentieth-century English writer before the sixties – Chekhov with an English accent; he's the first modern British director; he's the real founder of the National Theatre and, in his *Prefaces*, he's a man who, alone amongst Shakespearean commentators before Jan Kott, believed in the power of Shakespeare on stage.

There was a myth that Granville Barker was the natural son of Shaw. He was certainly someone whom Shaw could, in his awkward way, cherish and admire, educate and castigate. When Barker fell wildly in love ('in the Italian manner' as Shaw said) with Helen Huntington, an American millionairess, he married her, acquired a hyphen in his surname, moved first to Devon to play the part of a country squire, and then to France to a life of seclusion. Shaw thought that he had buried himself alive and could never reconcile himself to the loss. It was, as his biographer

Hesketh Pearson said: 'The only important matter about which he asked me to be reticent.'

After directing many of Shaw's plays for many years, acting many of his best roles (written by Shaw with Barker in mind), dreaming and planning together the birth of a National Theatre, not to mention writing, directing, and acting in his own plays while managing his own company at the Royal Court, Barker withdrew from the theatre, and for twenty years there was silence between the two men. Only on the occasion of the death of Shaw's wife did they communicate by letters. 'I did not know I could be so moved by anything,' wrote Shaw to him.

Out of this self-exile came one major work, slowly assembled over many years: *The Prefaces to Shakespeare*. With a few exceptions (Auden on *Othello*, Barbara Everett on *Hamlet*, Jan Kott on *The Tempest*) it's the only critical work about Shakespeare that's made any impact on me, apart, that is, from my father's view of Shakespeare, which was brief and brutal: 'It's absolute balls.'

As much as we need a good father, we need a good teacher. Mine, improbably perhaps, was Kingsley Amis. He'd arrived, somewhat diffidently, at Cambridge at the same time as I did. The depth of my ignorance of English literature corresponded almost exactly to his dislike of the theatre. Nevertheless, he made me see Shakespeare with a mind uncontaminated by the views of academics, whom he would never have described as his fellows and whose views he regarded as, well, academic. I would write essays marinated in the opinions of Spurgeon, Wilson Knight, Dover Wilson and a large cast of critical supernumeraries. He would gently, but courteously, cast aside my essay about, say, *Twelfth Night*: 'But what do *you* think of this play? Do you think it's any good?' 'Well ... er ... it's Shakespeare.' 'Yes, but is it any *good*? I mean as a *play*. It says it's a comedy. Fine. But does it have any decent jokes?'

I took this for irreverence, heresy even. Over the years, however, I've come to regard this as good teaching, or, closely allied, good direction. It's asking the right questions, unintimidated by reputation, by tradition, by received opinion, or by critical orthodoxy. This was shocking, but healthy, for a young and impressionable man ripe to become a fundamentalist in matters of literary taste and ready to revere F. R. Leavis as the Ayatollah of 'Cambridge English'. What you have is yourself and the text, only that. That's the lesson of Granville Barker: 'We have the text to guide us, half a dozen stage directions, and that is all. I abide by the text and the demands of the text and beyond that I claim freedom.' I can't imagine a more useful and more enduring dictum.

The Prefaces have a practical aim: 'I want to see Shakespeare made fully effective on the English stage. That is the best sort of help I can lend.' What Granville Barker wrote is a primer for directors and actors working on the plays of Shakespeare. There is lamentably little useful literature about the making of theatre, even though there is an indigestible glut of memoirs and biographies, largely concerned with events that have taken place *after* the curtain has fallen. If I was asked by a visiting Martian to recommend books which would help him, her or it to make theatre in the manner of the European I could only offer four books: Stanislavsky on *The Art of the Stage*, John Willett's *Brecht on Theatre*, Peter Brook's *The Empty Space*, and *The Prefaces to Shakespeare*.

Stanislavsky offers a pseudo-scientific dissection of the art of acting which is, in some respects, like reading Freud on the mechanism of the joke: earnest, well-meaning, but devoid of the indispensable ingredient of its subject matter: humour. Stanislavsky's great contribution was to demand that actors hold the mirror up to nature, that they take their craft as seriously as the writers they served, and to provide some sort of formal discipline within which both aims could be realised.

Brecht provided a manifesto that was a political and aesthetic response to the baroque encrustations of the scenery-laden, star-dominated, archaic boulevard theatre of Germany in the twenties. Although much of what he wrote as theory is an unpalatable mix of political ideology and artistic instruction, it is his theatrical instinct that prevails. He asserts, he insists, he browbeats. He demands that the stage, like society, must be re-examined, reformed, that the audience's habits mustn't be satisfied, they must be changed, but just when he is about to nail his 13 Articles to the church door he drops the voice of the zealot: 'The stage is not a hothouse or a zoological museum full of stuffed animals. It must be peopled with live, three-dimensional self-contradictory people with their passions, unconsidered utterances and actions.' In all art forms, he says, the guardians of orthodoxy will assert that there are eternal and immutable laws that you ignore at your peril, but in the theatre there is only one inflexible rule: 'The proof of the pudding is in the eating.' Brecht teaches us to ask the question: what goes on in a theatre?

Brook takes that question even further: what *is* theatre? It's a philosophical, but eminently practical, question that Brook has been asking for over 30 years and which has taken him to the African desert, a quarry in Iran, and an abandoned music hall in Paris. 'I take an empty space and call it a bare stage. A man walks across this empty space while someone else is watching him, and that is all that is needed for an act of theatre to be engaged.' For all his apparent concern with metaphyics, there is no more practical man of the theatre than Brook.

I was once at a seminar where someone asked him what was the job of the director. 'To get the actors on and off stage,' he said. Like Brecht, like Stanislavsky, like Granville Barker, Brook argues that for the theatre to be expressive it must be, above all, simple and unaffected: a distillation of language, of gesture, of action, of design, where meaning is the essence. The meaning must be felt as much as understood. 'They don't have to understand with their ears,' says Granville Barker, 'just with their guts.'

Brecht did not acknowledge a debt to Granville Barker. Perhaps he was not aware of one, but it seems to me that Barker's Shakespeare productions were the direct antecedents of Brecht's work. He certainly knew enough about English theatre to know that he was on to a good thing adapting *The Beggar's Opera*, *The Recruiting Officer* and *Coriolanus*. Brecht has been lauded for destroying illusionism; Granville Barker has been unhymned. He aimed at re-establishing the relationship between actor and audience that had existed in Shakespeare's theatre – and this at a time when the prevailing style of Shakespearean production involved *not* stopping short of having live sheep in *As You Like It*. He abolished footlights and the proscenium arch, building out an apron over the orchestra pit which Shaw said 'apparently trebled the spaciousness of the stage. . . . To the imagination it looks as if he had invented a new heaven and a new earth.'

His response to staging Shakespeare was not to look for a synthetic Elizabethanism. 'We shall not save our souls by being Elizabethan.' To recreate the Globe would, he knew, be aesthetic anasthaesia, involving the audience in an insincere conspiracy to pretend that they were willing collaborators in a vain effort to turn the clock back. His answers to staging Shakespeare were similar to Brecht's for *his* plays and, in some senses, to

Chekhov's for his. He wanted scenery not to decorate and be literal, but to be expressive and metaphorical, and at the same time, in apparent contradiction, to be specific and be real, while being minimal and iconographic: the cart in *Mother Courage*, the nursery in *The Cherry Orchard*, the dining table in *The Voysey Inheritance*. 'To create a new hieroglyphic language of scenery. That, in a phrase, is the problem. If the designer finds himself competing with the actors, the sole interpreters Shakespeare has licensed, then it is he that is the intruder and must retire.'

In *The Prefaces* Granville Barker argues for a fluency of staging unbroken by scene changes. Likewise the verse should be spoken fast. 'Be swift, be swift, be not poetical,' he wrote on the dressing-room mirror of Cathleen Nesbitt when she played Perdita. Within the speed, however, detailed reality. *Meaning* above all.

It is the director's task, with the actors, to illuminate the meanings of a play: its vocabulary, its syntax, and its philosophy. The director has to ask what each scene is revealing about the characters and their actions: what story is each scene telling us? In *The Prefaces* Granville Barker exhumes, examines and explains the lost stagecraft of Shakespeare line by line, scene by scene, play by play.

Directing Shakespeare is a matter of understanding the meaning of a scene and staging it in the light of that knowledge. Easier said than done, but it's at the heart of the business of directing any play, and directing Shakespeare is merely directing writ large. Beyond that, as David Mamet has observed, 'choice of actions and adverbs constitute the craft of directing'. Get up from that chair and walk across the room. Slowly.

With Shakespeare as with any other playwright the director's job is to make the play live, now, in the present tense. 'Spontaneous enjoyment is the life of the theatre,' says Granville Barker in his Preface to *Love's Labour's Lost*. To receive a review, as Granville Barker did, headed *SHAKESPEARE ALIVE!* is the most, but should be the least, that a director must hope for.

I regard Granville Barker not only as the first modern English director but as the most influential. Curiously, partly as a result of his early withdrawal from the theatre, partly because his *Prefaces* have been out of print for many years, and partly because of his own self-effacement, he has been unjustly ignored both in the theatre and in the academic world, where the codification of their 'systems' has resulted in the canonisation of Brecht and Stanislavsky. I hope the re-publication of *The Prefaces* will right the balance. Granville Barker himself always thought of them as his permanent legacy to the theatre.

My sense of filial identification is not entirely a professional one. When I directed *The Voysey Inheritance* I wanted a photograph of the author on the poster. A number of people protested that it was the height, or depth, of vanity and self-aggrandisement to put my own photograph on the poster. I was astonished, I was bewildered, but I was not unflattered. I still can't see the resemblance, but it's not through lack of trying.

Two years ago the Royal National Theatre was presented with a wonderful bronze bust of Granville Barker by Katherine Scott (the wife, incidentally, of the Antarctic hero). For a while it sat on the windowsill of my office like a benign household god. Then it was installed on a bracket in the foyer opposite a bust of Olivier, the two men eyeing each other in wary mutual regard. A few months later it was stolen; an act of homage perhaps. I miss him.

Richard Eyre

Introduction

We have still much to learn about Shakespeare the playwright. Strange that it should be so, after three centuries of commentary and performance, but explicable. For the Procrustean methods of a changed theatre deformed the plays, and put the art of them to confusion; and scholars, with this much excuse, have been apt to divorce their Shakespeare from the theatre altogether, to think him a poet whose use of the stage was quite incidental, whose glory had small relation to it, for whose lapses it was to blame.

The Study and the Stage

THIS much is to be said for Garrick and his predecessors and successors in the practice of reshaping Shakespeare's work to the theatre of their time. The essence of it was living drama to them, and they meant to keep it alive for their public. They wanted to avoid whatever would provoke question and so check that spontaneity of response upon which acted drama depends. Garrick saw the plays, with their lack of 'art', through the spectacles of contemporary culture; and the bare Elizabethan stage, if it met his mind's eye at all, doubtless as a barbarous makeshift. Shakespeare was for him a problem; he tackled it, from our point of view, misguidedly and with an overplus of enthusiasm. His was a positive world; too near in time, moreover, as well as too opposed in taste to Shakespeare's to treat it perspectively. The romantic movement might have brought a more concordant outlook. But by then the scholars were off their own way; while the theatre began to think of its Shakespeare from the point of view of the picturesque, and, later, in terms of upholstery. Nineteenth-century drama developed along the lines of realistic illusion, and the staging of Shakespeare was further subdued to this, with inevitably disastrous effect on the speaking of his verse; there was less perversion of text perhaps, but actually more wrenching of the construction of the plays for the convenience of the stage carpenter. The public appetite for this sort of thing having been gorged, producers then turned to newer—and older—contrivances, leaving 're- alism' (so called) to the modern comedy that had fa- thered it. Amid much vaporous theorizing—but let us humbly own how hard it is not to write nonsense about art, which seems ever pleading to be enjoyed and not written about at all—the surprising discovery had been made that varieties of stagecraft and stage were not historical accidents but artistic obligations, that Greek drama belonged in a Greek theatre, that Elizabethan plays, therefore, would, presumably, do best upon an Elizabethan stage, that there was nothing sacrosanct about scenery, footlights, drop-curtain or any of their belongings. This brings us to the present situation.

There are few enough Greek theatres in which Greek tragedy can be played; few enough people want to see it, and they will applaud it encouragingly however it is done. Some acknowledgement is due to the altruism of the doers! Shakespeare is another matter. The English theatre, doubtful of its destiny, of necessity venal, open- ing its doors to all comers, seems yet, as by some instinct, to seek renewal of strength in him. An actor, unless success has made him cynical, or his talent be merely trivial, may take some pride in the hall mark of Shakes- pearean achievement. So may a manager if he thinks he can afford it. The public (or their spokesmen) seem to consider Shakespeare and his genius a sort of national property, which, truly, they do nothing to conserve, but in which they have moral rights not lightly to be flouted. The production of the plays is thus still apt to be marked by a timid respect for 'the usual thing'; their acting is crippled by pseudo-traditions, which are inert because they are not Shakespearean at all. They are the accumulation of two centuries of progressive misconception and distortion of his playwright's art. On the other hand, England has been spared production of Shakespeare according to this or that even more irrelevant theory of presentationalism, symbolism, constructivism or what not. There is the breach in the wall of 'realism', but we have not yet made up our minds to pass through, taking our Shakespeare with us.

Incidentally, we owe the beginning of the breach to Mr William Poel, who, with fanatical courage, when 'realism' was at the tottering height of its triumph in the later revivals of Sir Henry Irving, and the yet more richly upholstered revelations of Sir Herbert Tree, thrust the Elizabethan stage in all its apparent eccentricity upon our unwilling notice.[1] Mr Poel shook complacency. He could not expect to do much more; for he was a logical reformer. He showed us the Elizabethan stage, with Antony and Cleopatra, Troilus and Cressida, in their ruffs and farthingales as for Shakespeare's audiences they lived. Q.E.D. There, however, as far as the popular theatre was concerned, the matter seemed to rest for twenty years or so. But it was just such a demonstration that was needed; anything less drastic and provocative might have been passed over with mild approval.

To get the balance true, let us admit that while Shakespeare was an Elizabethan playwright he was—and now is to us—predominantly something much more. Therefore we had better not too unquestioningly thrust him back within the confines his genius has escaped, nor presume him to have felt the pettier circumstances of his theatre sacrosanct. Nor can we turn Elizabethans as we watch the plays; and every mental effort to do so will subtract from our enjoyment of them. This is the case against the circumstantial reproduction of Shakespeare's staging. But Mr Poel's achievement remains; he cleared for us from Shakespeare's stagecraft the scenic rubbish by which it had been so long encumbered and disguised. And we could now, if we would, make a promising fresh start. For the scholars, on their side, have lately—the scholarly among them—cut clear of the transcendental fog (scenic illusion of another sort) in which their nine-teenth-century peers loved to lose themselves, and they too are beginning again at the beginning. A text acquires virtue now by its claim to be a prompt book, and the most comprehensive work of our time upon the Elizabe-than stage is an elaborate sorting-out of plays, companies and theatres. On Dr Pollard's treatment of the texts and on the foundations of fact laid by Sir Edmund Chambers a new scholarship is rising, aiming first to see Shakes-peare in the theatre for which he wrote. It is a scholar-ship, therefore, by which the theatre of today can profit, to which, by its acting of Shakespeare, it could contrib-ute, one would hope. Nor should the scholars disdain the help; for criticism cannot live upon criticism, it needs refreshment from the living art. Besides, what is all the criticism and scholarship finally for if not to keep Shakes-peare alive? And he must always be most alive—even if roughly and rudely alive—in the theatre. Let the scholars force a way in there, if need be. Its fervid atmosphere will do them good; the benefit will be mu-tual.

These Prefaces are an attempt to profit by this new scholarship and to contribute to it some research into Shakespeare's stagecraft, by examining the plays, one

after another, in the light of the interpretation he de-
signed for them, so far as this can be deduced; to discover,
if possible, the production he would have desired for
them, all merely incidental circumstances apart. They
might profit more written a generation hence, for the
ground they build upon is still far from clear. And this
introduction is by no means a conspectus of the subject;
that can only come as a sequel. There has been, in this
branch of Shakespearean study, too much generalization
and far too little analysis of material.[2]

Shakespeare's Stagecraft

SHAKESPEARE'S own career was not a long one. The
whole history of the theatre he wrote for does not cover
a century. Between Marlowe and Massinger, from the
first blaze to the glowing of the embers, it is but fifty
years. Yet even while Shakespeare was at work, the stage
to which he fitted his plays underwent constant and
perhaps radical change. From Burbage's first theatre to
the Globe, then to Blackfriars, not to mention excursions
to Court and into the great halls—change of audiences
and their behaviour, of their taste, development of the
art of acting, change of the stage itself and its resources
were all involved in the progress, and are all, we may
be sure, reflected to some degree in the plays themselves.
We guess at the conditions of each sort of stage and
theatre, but there is often the teasing question to which
of them had a play, as we have it now, been adapted.
And of the 'private' theatre, most in vogue for the ten
years preceding the printing of the First Folio so far we
know least. The dating of texts and their ascription to
the usages of a particular theatre may often be a search-
light upon their stagecraft. Here is much work for the
new scholarship.

Conversely, the watchful working-out of the plays in action upon this stage or that would be of use to the scholars, who otherwise must reconstruct their theatre and gloss their texts as in a vacuum. The play was once fitted to the stage; it is by no means impossible to rebuild that stage now, with its doors, balconies, curtains and machines, by measuring the needs of the play. It is idle, for instance, to imagine scenes upon inner or upper stage without evidence that they will be audible or visible there; and editing is still vitiated by lack of this simple knowledge. Here, if nowhere else, this present research must fall short, for its method should rightly be experimental; more than one mind should be at work on it, moreover.

The text of a play is a score waiting performance, and the performance and its preparation are, almost from the beginning, a work of collaboration. A producer may direct the preparation, certainly. But if he only knows how to give orders, he has mistaken his vocation; he had better be a drill-sergeant. He might talk to his company when they all met together for the first time to study *Love's Labour's Lost*, *Julius Cæsar* or *King Lear*, on some such lines as these Prefaces pursue, giving a considered opinion of the play, drawing a picture of it in action, providing, in fact, a hypothesis which mutual study would prove—and might partly disprove. No sort of study of a play can better the preparation of its performance if this is rightly done. The matured art of the playwright lies in giving life to characters in action, and the secret of it in giving each character a due chance in the battle, the action of a play becoming literally the fighting of a battle of character. So the greater the playwright, the wider and deeper his sympathies, the more genuine this opposition will be and the less easily will a single mind grasp it, as it must be grasped, in the fullness of its emotion. The dialogue of a play runs—and often intricately—upon lines of reason, but it is charged besides with an emotion which speech releases, yet only releases fully when the speaker is—as an actor is—identified with the character. There is further the incidental action, implicit in the dialogue, which springs to life only when a scene is in being. A play, in fact, as we find it written, is a magic spell; and even the magician cannot always foresee the full effect of it.

Not every play, it must be owned, will respond to such intensive study. Many, ambitiously conceived, would collapse under the strain. Many are mere occasions for display of their actors' wit or eloquence, good looks or nice behaviour, and meant to be no more; and if they are skilfully contrived the parts fit together and the whole machine should go like clockwork. Nor, in fact, are even the greatest plays often so studied. There is hardly a theatre in the world where masterpiece and trumpery alike are not rushed through rehearsals to an arbitrarily effective performance, little more learned of them than the words, gaps in the understanding of them filled up with 'business'—effect without cause, the demand for this being the curse of the theatre as of other arts, as of other things than art. Not to such treatment will the greater plays of Shakespeare yield their secrets. But working upon a stage which reproduced the essential conditions of his, working as students, not as showmen merely, a company of actors might well find many of the riddles of the library answering themselves unasked. And these Prefaces could best be a record of such work, if such work were to be done.

We cannot, on the other hand, begin our research by postulating the principles of the Elizabethan stage. One is tempted to say it had none, was too much a child of nature to bother about such things. Principles were

8

doubtless imposed upon it when it reached respectability, and heads would be bowed to the yoke. Shakespeare's among them? He had served a most practical apprenticeship to his trade. If he did not hold horses at the door, he sat behind the curtains, we may be sure, and held the prompt book on occasion. He acted, he cobbled other men's plays, he could write his own to order. Such a one may stay a journeyman if he is not a genius, but he will not become a doctrinaire. Shakespeare's work shows such principles as the growth of a tree shows. It is not haphazard merely because it is not formal; it is shaped by inner strength. The theatre, as he found it, allowed him and encouraged him to great freedom of development. Because the material resources of a stage are simple, it does not follow that the technique of its playwriting will stay so. Crude work may show up more crudely, when there are none of the fal-lals of illusion to disguise it that the modern theatre provides. But, if he has it in him, a dramatist can, so unfettered, develop the essentials of his art more boldly and more subtly too. The Elizabethan drama made an amazingly quick advance from crudity to an excellence which was often technically most elaborate. The advance and the not less amazing gulf which divides its best from its worst may be ascribed to the simplicity of the machinery it employed. That its decadence was precipitated by the influence of the Masque and the shifting of its centre of interest from the barer public stage to the candle-lit private theatre, where the machinery of the Masque became effective, it would be rash to assert; but the occurrences are suspiciously related. Man and machine (here at any rate is a postulate, if a platitude!) are false allies in the theatre, secretly at odds; and when man gets the worst of it, drama is impoverished; and the struggle, we may add, is perennial. No great drama depends upon pageantry. All great drama tends to concentrate upon character; and, even so, not upon picturing men as they show themselves to the world like figures on a stage—though that is how it must ostensibly show them—but on the hidden man. And the progress of Shakespeare's art from *Love's Labour's Lost* to *Hamlet*, and thereafter with a difference, lies in the simplifying of this paradox and the solving of the problem it presents; and the process involves the developing of a very subtle sort of stagecraft indeed.

For one result we have what we may call a very self-contained drama. Its chief values, as we know, have not changed with the fashions of the theatre. It relies much on the music of the spoken word, and a company of schoolchildren with pleasant voices, and an ear for rhythm, may vociferate through a play to some effect. It is as much to be enjoyed in the reading, if we hear it in imagination as we read, as drama meant to be acted can be. As with its simplicities then, so it should be, we presume, with its complexities. The subtly emotional use of verse and the interplay of motive and character, can these not be appreciated apart from the bare boards of their original setting? It does not follow. It neither follows that the advantages of the Elizabethan stage were wholly negative nor that, with our present knowledge, we can imagine the full effect of a play in action upon it. The imagining of a play in action is, under no circumstances, an easy thing.[3] What would one not give to go backward through the centuries to see the first performance of *Hamlet*, played as Shakespeare had it played![4] In default, if we could but make ourselves read it as if it were a manuscript fresh from its author's hands! There is much to be said for turning one's back on the editors, even, when possible, upon the First Folio with its demarcation of acts and scenes, in favour of the Quartos—Dr Pollard's 'good' Quartos—in their yet greater simplicity.

The Convention of Place

IT is, for instance, hard to discount the impression made merely by reading: *Scene i—Elsinore. A platform before the Castle*; and most of us have, to boot, early memories of painted battlements and tenth-century castles (of ageing Hamlets and their portly mothers for that matter) very difficult to dismiss. No great harm, one protests; it was a help, perhaps, to the unimaginative. But it is a first step to the certain misunderstanding of Shakespeare's stagecraft. The 'if, how and when' of the presenting of localities on the Elizabethan stage is, of course, a complex question. Shakespeare himself seems to have followed, consciously, no principles in the matter, nor was his practice very logical, nor at all consistent. It may vary with the play he is writing and the particular stage he is writing for; it will best be studied in relation to each play. We can, however, free ourselves from one general misconception which belongs to our own over-logical standpoint. When we learn with a shock of surprise—having begun in the schoolroom upon the Shakespeare of the editors, it comes as belated news to us—that neither battlements, throne rooms nor picturesque churchyards were to be seen at the Globe, and that *Elsinore. A platform before the Castle* is not Shakespeare at all, we yet imagine ourselves among the audience there busily conjuring these things up before the eye of faith. The Elizabethan audience was at no such pains. Nor was this their alternative to seeing the actors undisguisedly concerned with the doors, curtains and balconies which, by the play's requirements, should have been anything but what they were. As we, when a play has no hold on us, may fall to thinking about the scenery, so to a Globe audience, unmoved, the stage might be an obvious bare stage. But are we conscious of the scenery behind the actor when the play really moves us? If we are, there is something very wrong with the scenery, which should know its place as a background. The audience was not conscious of curtain and balcony when Burbage played Hamlet to them. They were conscious of Hamlet. That conventional background faded as does our painted illusion, and they certainly did not deliberately conjure up in its place mental pictures of Elsinore. The genus audience is passive, if expectant, imaginatively lazy till roused, never, one may be sure, at pains to make any effort that is generally unnecessary to enjoyment.

With Shakespeare the locality of a scene has dramatic importance, or it has none; and this is as true of his early plays as his late ones. Both in *Richard II* and *Antony and Cleopatra*, scene after scene passes with no exact indication of where we may be. With *Cleopatra* we are surely in Egypt, with Cæsar in Rome. Pompey appears, and the talk tells us that both Egypt and Rome are elsewhere; but positively where Pompey is at the moment we never learn.[5] Indoors or outdoors? The action of the scene or the clothing of the characters will tell us this if we need to know. But, suddenly transported to the Parthian war, our whereabouts is made amply plain. It is, however, made plain by allusion. The information peeps out through talk of kindred things; we are hardly aware we are being told, and, again, we learn no more than we need to learn. This, truly, is a striking development from the plump and plain

> Barkloughly Castle call they this at hand?

of Richard II, even from the more descriptive

> I am a stranger here in Gloucestershire:
> These high wild hills and rough, uneven ways
> Draw out our miles. . .

by which Shakespeare pictures and localizes the manoeuvres of Richard and Bolingbroke when he wants to.
But the purpose is the same, and the method essentially
the same.[6] Towards the end of the later play come scene
after scene of the marching and countermarching of
armies, of fighting, of truce, all the happenings of three
days' battle. Acts III and IV contain twenty-eight scenes
long and short; some of them are very short; three of
them have but four lines apiece. The editors conscientiously ticket them *A plain near Actium, Another part of the
plain, Another part of the plain* and so on, and conclude that
Shakespeare is really going too far and too fast, is indeed
(I quote Sir Edmund Chambers) 'in some danger of
outrunning the apprehensions of his auditory.' Indeed he
might be if this cinematographic view of his intentions
were the right one! But it utterly falsifies them. Show an
audience such a succession of painted scenes—if you
could at the pace required—and they would give attention to nothing else whatever; the drama would pass
unnoticed. Had Shakespeare tried to define the whereabouts of every scene in any but the baldest phrases—the
protesting editors seem not to see that he makes no
attempt to; only *they* do!—he would have had to lengthen
and complicate them; had he written only a labelling
line or two he would still have distracted his audience
from the essential drama. Ignoring whereabouts, letting
it at most transpire when it naturally will, the characters
capture all attention. This is the true gain of the bare
stage; unless to some dramatic end no precious words
need be spent, in complying with the undramatic demands of space and time; incarnation of character can
be all in all. Given such a crisis as this the gain is yet
greater. We are carried through the phases of the three
days' battle; and what other stage convention would
allow us so varied a view of it, could so isolate the true

drama of it? For do we not pass through such a crisis
in reality with just that indifference to time and place?
These scenes, in their kind, show Shakespeare's stagecraft, not at its most reckless, but at its very best, and
exemplify perfectly the freedom he enjoyed that the stage
of visual illusion has inevitably lost. His drama is at-
tached solely to its actors and their acting; that, perhaps,
puts it in a phrase. They carry place and time with them
as they move. The modern theatre still accepts the
convention that measures time more or less by a play's
convenience; a half-hour stands for an hour or more,
and we never question the vagary. It was no more
strange to an Elizabethan audience to see a street in
Rome turned, in the use made of it, to the Senate House
by the drawing of a curtain and the disclosure of
Cæsar's state, to find Cleopatra's Monument now on the
upper stage because Antony had to be drawn up to it,
later on the lower because Cleopatra's death-scene could
best be played there; it would seem that they were not
too astonished even when Juliet, having taken leave of
Romeo on the balcony of her bedroom and watched him
descend to the lower stage, the scene continuing, came
down, a few lines later, to the lower stage herself,
bringing, so to speak, her bedroom with her—since this
apparently is what she must have done.[7] For neither
Senate House, Monument nor balcony had rights and
reality of their own. They existed for the convenience
of the actors, whose touch gave them life, a shadowy life
at most; neglected, they existed no longer.[8]

Shakespeare's stagecraft concentrates, and inevitably,
upon opportunity for the actor. We think now of the
plays themselves; their first public knew them by their
acting; and the development of the actor's art from the
agilities and funniments of the clown, and from round-
mouthed rhetoric to imaginative interpreting of character

by such standards as Hamlet set up for his players, was a factor in the drama's triumph that we now too often ignore. Shakespeare himself, intent more and more upon plucking out the heart of the human mystery, stimulated his actors to a poignancy and intimacy of emotional expression—still can stimulate them to it—as no other playwright has quite learned to do.

The Speaking of the Verse

His verse was, of course, his chief means to this emotional expression; and when it comes to staging the plays, the speaking of verse must be the foundation of all study. The changes of three hundred years have of themselves put difficulties in our way here; though there are some besides—as one imagines—of Shakespeare's own making. Surely his syntax must now and then have puzzled even his contemporaries. Could they have made much more than we can of Leontes'

> Affection! thy intention stabs the centre;
> Thou dost make possible things not so held,
> Communicat'st with dreams;—How can this be?
> With what's unreal thou coactive art,
> And fellow'st nothing; then, 'tis very credent
> Thou may'st co-join with something; and thou dost;
> And that beyond commission; and I find it,
> And that to the infection of my brains,
> And hardening of my brows.

The confusion of thought and intricacy of language is dramatically justified. Shakespeare is picturing a genuinely jealous man (the sort of man that Othello was *not*) in the grip of a mental epilepsy. We parse the passage and dispute its sense; spoken, as it was meant to be, in a choking torrent of passion, probably a modicum of sense slipped through, and its first hearers did not find it a mere rigmarole. But we are apt to miss even that much. Other passages, of early and late writing, may always have had as much sound as sense to them; but now, to the casual hearer, they will convey more sound than sense by far. Nor do puns mean to us what they meant to the Elizabethans, delighting in their language for its own sake. Juliet's tragic fantasia upon 'Aye' and 'I' sounds all but ridiculous, and one sympathizes with an actress hesitating to venture on it. How far, apart from the shifting of accents and the recolouring of vowels, has not the whole habit of English speech changed in these three hundred years? In the theatre it was slowing down, one fancies, throughout the eighteenth century; and in the nineteenth, as far as Shakespeare was concerned, it grew slower and slower, till on occasions one thought—even hoped—that shortly the actor would stop altogether. There may have been more than one cause; imitation of the French Augustans, the effort to make antiquated phrases understood, the increasing size of the theatres themselves would all contribute to it. The result, in any case, is disastrous. Elizabethan drama was built upon vigour and beauty of speech. The groundlings may often have deserved Shakespeare's strictures, but they would stand in discomfort for an hour or so to be stirred by the sound of verse. Some of the actors no doubt were robustious periwigpated fellows, but, equally, it was no empty ideal of acting he put into Hamlet's mouth—and Burbage's. We may suppose that at its best the mere speaking of the plays was a very brilliant thing, compared to *bel canto*, or to a pianist's virtuosity. The emotional appeal of our modern music was in it, and it could be tested by ears trained to the rich and delicate fretwork of the music of that day. Most Hamlets—not being playwrights—make a mild joke of telling us they'd as lief the town-crier spoke their lines, but we may hear in it the echo of some of Shakespeare's sorest trials.

The speaking of his verse must be studied, of course, in relation to the verse's own development. The actor must not attack its supple complexities in *Antony and Cleopatra* and *Cymbeline*, the mysterious dynamics of *Macbeth*, the nobilities of *Othello*, its final pastoral simplicities in *A Winter's Tale* and *The Tempest* without preliminary training in the lyricism, the swift brilliance and the masculine clarity of the earlier plays. A modern actor, alas, thinks it simple enough to make his way, splay-footed, through

> The cloud-capped towers, the gorgeous palaces...

though Berowne's

> I, forsooth, in love...

or one of Oberon's apostrophes will defeat him utterly. And, without an ear trained to the delicacy of the earlier work, his hearers, for their part, will never know how shamefully he is betraying the superb ease of the later. If we are to make Shakespeare our own again we must all be put to a little trouble about it. We must recapture as far as may be his lost meanings; and the sense of a phrase we *can* recapture, though instinctive emotional response to it may be a loss forever. The tunes that he writes to, the whole great art of his music-making, we can master. Actors can train their ears and tongues and can train our ears to it. We talk of lost arts. No art is ever lost while the means to it survive. Our faculties rust by disuse and by misuse are coarsened, but they quickly recover delight in a beautiful thing. Here, at any rate, is the touchstone by which all interpreting of Shakespeare the playwright must first—and last—be tried.

The Boy-Actress

MORE than one of the conditions of his theatre made this medium of accomplished speech of such worth to him. Boys played the women parts; and what could a boy bring to Juliet, Rosalind or Cleopatra beyond grace of manner and charm of speech? We have been used to women on the stage for two hundred and fifty years or more, and a boy Juliet—if the name on the programme revealed one, for nothing else might—would seem an odd fish to us; no one would risk a squeaking Cleopatra; though, as for Rosalind, through three-parts of the play a boy would have the best of it. But the parts were written for boys; not, therefore, without consideration of how boys could act them most convincingly. Hence, of course, the popularity of the heroine so disguised. The disguise was perfect; the make-believe one degree more complex, certainly, than it needs to be with us; but once you start make-believe it matters little how far you go with it; there is, indeed, some enjoyment in the make-believe itself. But, further, it is Shakespeare's constant care to demand nothing of a boy-actress that might turn to unseemliness or ridicule. He had not much taste for what is called 'domestic drama,' nor does he dose us very heavily with Doll Tearsheet, Mistress Overdone and their like. Constance mourns Arthur's loss, Lady Macduff has her little son, but no mother croons over the child in her arms. Paulina brings Hermione's baby to Leontes, it is true; but see with what tact, from this point of view, the episode is managed. And love-scenes are most carefully contrived. Romeo and Juliet are seldom alone together; never for long, but in the balcony-scene; and in this, the most famous of love-scenes, they are kept from all contact with each other. Consider *Antony and*

Cleopatra. Here is a tragedy of sex without one single scene of sexual appeal. That aspect of Cleopatra is reflected for us in talk about her; mainly by Enobarbus, who is not mealymouthed; but his famed description of her voluptuousness is given us when she has been out of our sight for several scenes. The play opens with her parting from Antony, and in their two short encounters we see her swaying him by wit, malice and with the moods of her mind. Not till the story takes its tragic plunge and sex is drowned in deeper passion are they ever intimately together; till he is brought to her dying there has been occasion for but one embrace. Contrast this with a possible Cleopatra planned to the advantage of the actress of today.

Shakespeare, artist that he was, turned this limitation to account, made loss into a gain.[9] Feminine charm—of which the modern stage makes such capital—was a medium denied him. So his men and women encounter upon a plane where their relation is made rarer and intenser by poetry, or enfranchised in a humour which surpasses more primitive love-making. And thus, perhaps, he was helped to discover that the true stuff of tragedy and of the liveliest comedy lies beyond sensual bounds. His studies of women seem often to be begun from some spiritual paces beyond the point at which a modern dramatist leaves off. Curious that not a little of the praise lavished upon the beauty and truth of them—mainly by women—may be due to their having been written to be played by boys!

Much could be said for the restoring of the celibate stage; but the argument, one fears, would be academic. Here, though, is practical counsel. Let the usurping actress remember that her sex is a liability, not an asset. The dramatist of today may refuse to exploit its allurements, but may legitimately allow for the sympathetic effect of it; though the less he does so, perhaps, the better for his play and the more gratitude the better sort of actress will show him. But Shakespeare makes no such demands, has left no blank spaces for her to fill with her charm. He asks instead for self-forgetful clarity of perception, and for a sensitive, spirited, athletic beauty of speech and conduct, which will leave prettiness and its lures at a loss, and the crudities of more Circean appeal looking very crude indeed.

The Soliloquy

THIS convention of the boy-actress may be said to give a certain remoteness to a play's acting. The soliloquy brings a compensating intimacy, and its use was an important part of Shakespeare's stagecraft. Its recognized usefulness was for the disclosing of the plot, but he soon improved upon this. Soliloquy becomes the means by which he brings us not only to a knowledge of the more secret thoughts of his characters, but into the closest emotional touch with them too. Here the platform stage helped him, as the stage of scenic illusion now defeats his purpose. But it is not altogether a question of 'realism' and the supposed obligation this lays upon a real man in a real-looking room to do nothing he would not do if the whole affair were real.

There is no escape from convention in the theatre, and all conventions can be made acceptable, though they cannot all be used indiscriminately, for they are founded in the physical conditions of the stage of their origin and are often interdependent one with another. Together they form a code, and they are as a treaty made with the audience. No article of it is to be abrogated unless we can be persuaded to consent, and upon its basis we surrender our imaginations to the playwright.

With the soliloquy upon the platform stage it is a
case—as so often where convention is concerned—of
extremes meeting. There is no illusion, so there is every
illusion. Nothing very strange about this man, not even
the dress he wears, leaning forward a little we could
touch him; we are as intimate and familiar with him as
it is possible to be. We agree to call him 'Hamlet', to
suppose that he is where he says he is, we admit that
he thinks aloud and in blank verse too. It is possible that
the more we are asked to imagine the easier we find it
to do. It is certain that, once our imagination is working,
visual illusion will count for little in the stimulating of
emotion beside this intimacy that allows the magnetism
of personality full play.

There is no more important task for the producer of
Shakespeare than to restore to the soliloquy its rightful
place in a play's economy, and in particular to regain for
it full emotional effect. We now accept the convention
frigidly, the actor manoeuvres with it timidly. Banished
behind footlights into that other world of illusion, the
solitary self-communing figure rouses our curiosity at best.
Yet further adapted to the self-contained methods of
modern acting, the soliloquy has quite inevitably become
a slack link in the play's action, when it should be a
recurring reinforcement to its strength. Shakespeare never
pinned so many dramatic fortunes to a merely utilitarian
device. Time and again he may be feeling his way
through a scene for a grip on his audience, and it is the
soliloquy ending it that will give him—and his actor—the
stranglehold. When he wishes to quicken the pulse of
the action, to screw up its tension in a second or so, the
soliloquy serves him well. For a parallel to its full effec-
tiveness on Shakespeare's stage we should really look to
the modern music-hall comedian getting on terms with
his audience. We may measure the response to Burbage's

O, that this too too solid flesh would melt . . .

by recalling—those of us that happily can—Dan Leno as a washerwoman, confiding domestic troubles to a theatre full of friends, and taken unhindered to their hearts. The problem is not really a difficult one. If we solve the physical side of it by restoring, in essentials, the relation between actor and audience that the intimacy of the platform stage provided, the rest should soon solve itself.

Costume

THE problem of costume, when it arises, is a subtler one; nor probably is it capable of any logical solution. Half the plays can be quite appropriately dressed in the costume of Shakespeare's own time. It is a false logic which suggests that to match their first staging we should dress them in the costume of ours. For with costume goes custom and manners—or the lack of them. It may be both a purge and a tonic to the sluggish-fancied spectator to be shown a Prince of Denmark in coat and trousers and a Grave-digger in a bowler hat, for reminder that here is a play, not a collection of ritualized quotations. But physic is for the sick; also, there may be less drastic cures. When archaeology took hold upon the nineteenth-century mind it became a matter of moment to lodge Hamlet in historic surroundings; and withers were wrung by the anachronisms of ducats and a murder of Gonzago, French rapiers and the rest. A needlessly teasing difficulty; why reproduce it in terms of a young man in a dinner jacket searching for a sword—a thing not likely to be lying about in his modern mother's sitting room—with which to kill Polonius, who certainly has window curtains to hide behind instead of arras? This gain of intimacy—with a Hamlet we might find sitting opposite at a dinner party—may well be a gain in sympathy. It was originally a great gain, a gift to Shakespeare's audience. But we pay too high a price for it.

What was the actual Elizabethan practice in this matter of costuming is not comprehensively known. We can only say safely that, as with other matters, it was neither constant, consistent, nor, from our present point of view, rational. It was based upon the use of the clothes of the time; but these might be freely and fantastically adapted to suit a particular play or advantage some character in it. Dramatic effect was probably the first consideration and the last. There were such fancy dresses as Oberon or Puck or Caliban might wear; there was always the symbolizing of royalty, and a king would wear a crown whenever he could; there was the utility of knowing Romans from Britons by sight in *Cymbeline*, the martial Roman from the effete Egyptian in *Antony and Cleopatra*, and a Scottish lord when you saw him in *Macbeth*, if we may judge by Malcolm's comment upon Rosse's appearance:

> My countryman; and yet I know him not.

Our difficulty, of course, arises mainly over the historical plays. Not over the English Histories, even so; we can dress Richard III or Henry V by the light of our own superior knowledge of what they wore, and never find it clash violently with anything Shakespeare has put on their backs or in their mouths. But when we come to Julius Cæsar plucking open his doublet, to the conspirators against him with their hats about their ears, and to Cleopatra's

> Cut my lace, Charmian.

not to mention British Imogen in her doublet and hose, we must stop and consider.

The common practice is, in these instances, to ignore the details of Shakespeare's text altogether; to dress Cæsar in his toga, Cleopatra in her habit as she lived, with never a stay-lace about her (though, truly, the costumier, let alone, will tend to get his fashion a few thousand years wrong and turn her out more like the wife of Tutankhamen); and as to Imogen and her sur-roundings, we do our best to compromise with skins and woad. This may be a lesser evil than presenting a Cæsar recalling Sir Walter Raleigh and a Cleopatra who would make us think of Mary Queen of Scots, but it is no solution of the problem. For the actors have to speak these lines, and if action and appearance contradict them, credibility is destroyed. And the constant credi-bility of the actor must be a producer's first care. Nor is this all, nor is it, perhaps, the most important thing to consider. The plays are full of reference, direct and indirect, to Elizabethan custom. They are, further, im-pregnated with what we call 'Renaissance feeling', some more, some less, but all to a degree. Now of this last we have a sense which is likelier to be a better help to their appreciation than any newfangled knowledge of the correct cut of Cleopatra's clothes will be! We know Iago for a Machiavellian figure (so called), and miss none of Shakespeare's intention. But if ever two men breathed the air of a sixteenth-century court, Hamlet and Clau-dius of Denmark do, and to relate them in habit and behaviour to the twilight figures of Saxo Grammaticus is as much a misinterpretation as any mauling of the text can be. They exist essentially doubtless—as do all the major characters of the plays—in their perennial humanity. But never let us forget the means by which this deeper truth of them is made vivid and actual. There have been better intellects than Shakespeare's, and poetry as good as his. He holds his supreme place by his dramatist's necessary power of bringing thought and vague emotion to the terms of action and convincing speech; further, and far more than is often allowed, by his peculiar gift of bringing into contribution the common-place traffic of life. However wide the spoken word may range, there must be the actor, anchored to the stage. However high, then, with Shakespeare, the thought or emotion may soar, we shall always find the transcendental set in the familiar. He keeps this balance constantly adjusted; and, at his play's greatest moments, when he must make most sure of our response, he will employ the simplest means. The higher arguments of the plays are thus kept always within range, and their rooted humanity blossoms in a fertile upspringing of expressive little things. Neglect or misinterpret these, the inner wealth of Shakespeare will remain, no doubt, and we may mine for it, but we shall have levelled his landscape bare.

Shakespeare's own attitude in this matter of costume and customs was as inconsistent as his practice was casual. He knew what *his* Cæsar or Cleopatra would be wearing and would casually drop in a reference to it. Yet the great Romans themselves were aliens to him. The great idea of Rome fired his imagination. Brutus, Cassius and Antony do not turn typical Elizabethan gentlemen; and to the end of that play he is striving to translate Plutarch. Whenever, on the other hand, even for a moment he has made a character all his own, he cannot but clothe it in lively familiar detail. Cleopatra's are the coquetries of a great lady of his own time, in their phrasing, in the savour. When the heights of the tragedy have to be scaled, manners will not so much matter. But if we make her, at the play's beginning, a pseudo-classic, languishing Oriental, we must do it in spite of Shakespeare, not by his help. What then is the solution of this problem, if the sight of the serpent of old Nile in a farthingale will too dreadfully offend us? We can compromise. Look at Tintoretto's and Paolo Veronese's paintings of 'classic' subjects. We accept them readily enough.

Sometimes, within the boundaries of a play, the centuries seem all at odds. *Cymbeline* need not trouble us, its Roman Britain is pure 'once upon a time'. But in *King Lear*, for instance, Shakespeare is at unwonted pains to throw us back into some heathen past. Yet Edmund is another Iago, Edgar might have been at Wittenberg with Hamlet, and Oswald steps straight from the seventeenth-century London streets. Here, though, the dominant barbarism is the important thing; the setting for Goneril and Regan, Lear's tyranny and madness, and Gloucester's blinding. To a seventeenth-century audience Oswald was so identifiable a figure that it would not matter greatly how he dressed; the modern designer of costume must show him up as best he may. Each play, in fine, if it presents a problem at all, presents its own.

The Integrity of the Text

THE text, one says at first blush, can present no problem at all. The plays should be acted as Shakespeare wrote them—how dispute it? They should be; and it is as well, before we discuss hard cases, to have the principle freely admitted. Lip service enough is done it nowadays, and Colley Cibber's *Richard III*, Tate's *Lear* and Garrick's improvements are at the back of our bookshelves, but we still find Messrs John Doe and Richard Roe slicing out lines by the dozen and even a scene or so, or chopping and changing them to suit their scenery. This will not do. Shakespeare was not a perfect playwright; there can be no such thing. Nor did he aim at a mechanical perfection, but a vitality, and this he achieved. At best then, we cut and carve the body of a play to its peril. It may be robustly, but it may be very delicately organized. And we still know little enough of the laws of its existence, and some of us, perhaps, are not such very skilful surgeons; nor is any surgeon to be recommended who operates for his own convenience.

This good rule laid down, what are the exceptions that go to prove it? There is the pornographic difficulty. This is not such a stumbling block to us as it was to Bowdler, to some bright young eyes nowadays it is quite imperceptible, in fact. Yet, saving their presence, it exists; for it exists aesthetically. Shakespeare's characters often make obscene jokes. The manners of his time permitted it. The public manners of ours still do not. Now the dramatic value of a joke is to be measured by its effect upon an audience, and each is meant to make its own sort of effect. If then, instead of giving them a passing moment's amusement, it makes a thousand people uncomfortable and for the next five minutes very self-conscious, it fails of its true effect. This argument must not be stretched to cover the silliness of turning 'God' into 'Heaven' and of making Othello call Desdemona a 'wanton' (the practice, as I recollect, of the eighteen-nineties), nor to such deodorizing of *Measure for Measure* that it becomes hard to discover what all the fuss is about. If an audience cannot think of Angelo and the Duke, Pompey and Lucio, Isabella and Mistress Overdone, and themselves to boot, as fellow-creatures all, the play is not for them. Othello must call Desdemona a 'whore', and let those that do not like it leave the theatre; what have such queasy minds to do with the pity and terror of her murder and his death? Again, to make Beatrice so mealymouthed that she may not tell us how the devil is to meet her at the gates of hell, 'like an old cuckold with horns on his head', is to dress her in a crinoline, not a farthingale. But suppression of a few of the more scabrous jokes will not leave a play much the poorer; nor, one may add, will the average playgoer be much the wiser or merrier for hearing them, since they are often quite hard to understand.

Topical passages are a similar difficulty. With their savour, if not their very meaning lost, they show like dead wood in the living tree of the dialogue and are better, one would suppose, cut away. But no hard and fast rule will apply. Macbeth's porter's farmer and equivocator will never win spontaneous laughter again. But we cannot away with them, or nothing is left of the porter. Still the baffled low comedian must not, as his wont is, obscure the lines with bibulous antics. There will be that little dead spot in the play, and nothing can be done about it. Rosencrantz' reference to the 'eyrie of children' is meaningless except to the student. Is the play the poorer for the loss of it? But the logic that will take this out had better not rob us of

> Dead shepherd, now I find thy saw of might;
> Who ever loved that loved not at first sight?

And there is the strange case of

The lady of the Strachy married the yeoman of the wardrobe.

Nobody knows what it means, but everybody finds it funny when it is spoken in its place. And this has its parallels.

In general, however, better play the plays as we find them. The blue pencil is a dangerous weapon; and its use grows on a man, for it solves too many little difficulties far too easily.

Lastly, for a golden rule, whether staging or costuming or cutting is in question, and a comprehensive creed, a producer might well pin this on his wall: Gain Shakespeare's effects by Shakespeare's means when you can; for, plainly, this will be the better way. But gain Shakespeare's effects; and it is your business to discern them.

1927

Notes

1 But it should not be forgotten that Sir Herbert Tree, happy in the orthodoxy of public favour, welcomed the heretic Mr Poel more than once to a share in his Shakespeare Festivals.

2 I do not deal in general therefore with certain vexed questions, such as act-division, which still need to be looked at, I think, in the light of the particular play.

3 I remember a most intelligent reader of a modern play missing the whole point of a scene through which the chief character was to sit conspicuously and eloquently silent. He counted only with the written dialogue. I remember, when I thought I knew *King Lear* well enough, being amazed at the effect, all dialogue apart, of the mere meeting, when I saw it, of blind Gloucester and mad Lear.

4 Though, in a sense, there was no first performance of *Hamlet*. And doubtless many of the audience for Shakespeare's new version of the old play only thought he had spoiled a good story of murder and revenge by adding too much talk to it.

5 Unless it may be said that we learn in the scene after whereabouts he *was*.

6 And in *Coriolanus*, which probably postdates *Antony and Cleopatra*, with Marcius' 'A goodly city is this Antium,' we are back to the barely informative. It serves Shakespeare's purpose; he asks no more.

7 I fancy, though, that the later Shakespeare would have thought this a clumsy device.

8 How far this is true of other dramatists than Shakespeare I do not pretend to say; nor how far, with him, the influence of the private theatre, making undoubtedly towards the scenic stage

and (much later) for illusion, did not modify his practice, when he had that stage to consider. A question, again, for the bibliographers and historians.

9   There is no evidence, of course, that he felt it a loss, no such reference to the insufficiency of the boy-actress as there is to the overself-sufficiency of the clown. Women did appear in the Masques, if only to dance, so the gulf to be bridged was not a broad one. But the Elizabethan was as shocked by the notion of women appearing upon the public stage as the Chinese playgoer is today.

Antony and Cleopatra

HERE is the most spacious of the plays. It may lack the spiritual intimacy of *Hamlet*, the mysterious power of *Macbeth*, the nobilities of *Othello*, may reach neither to the heights nor depths of *King Lear*; but it has a magnificence and a magic all its own, and Shakespeare's eyes swept no wider horizon.

Eight years or so earlier he had written *Julius Cæsar*. There already are these rivals Antony and Octavius, comrades then; and the main clash of fortune and character is between Antony and Brutus, between the man of action and the idealist. Antony comes from it victorious; the tragedy is the soul's tragedy of Brutus. Thereafter Shakespeare gives us play after play upon this theme of the self-torturing soul. Hamlet (its chief exemplar), Othello, Macbeth, Lear are all concerned with the world within themselves. Now he returns to the world of great affairs, and, almost as if for emphasis, to the very pair that he left standing over the dead body of the idealist in defeat.[1]

We have a play of action, then, not of spiritual insight; that is the first thing to mark. Of a large field of action too. For if with *Julius Cæsar* the insularity of the earlier Histories was left behind, we are shown now not Rome in her might only, but the whole range of the Empire, eastward to Athens, Egypt and the Parthian bounds. Antony, the once-triumphant man of action, is hero; we are to watch his defeat by his subtler sometime pupil. Truly it is his passion for Cleopatra that is his ruin, and the action pulses to this; but the wider issue dictates form, method and the bulk of the play's content.

A tragedy of disillusion, we might call it. As to the lovers, from the beginning they have little to learn about each other.

> She is cunning past man's thought.

says Antony; and Cleopatra is very soon lashing at him with

> O most false love!
> Where be the sacred vials thou shouldst fill
> With sorrowful water? Now I see, I see,
> In Fulvia's death, how mine received shall be.

(though the event belies her). But the whole picture is shaded to this sere hue. 'My son,' said Oxenstierne, 'you will be amazed to discover with how little wisdom the world is governed.' We may sit through this play and add, 'With how little honour or honesty or decency either!' Shakespeare had not idealized the earlier Antony, nor—though the sketch of him is so slight—underrated Octavius.[2] But the dead Cæsar's champion was at least a gallant fellow, able and alert. In his stead we now see

> The triple pillar of the world transformed
> Into a strumpet's fool.

And that industrious apprentice Octavius, as he nears his reward, grows under our eyes ever colder of heart, more meanly calculating, more deliberately false. We meet Lepidus again, the 'barren-spirited fellow,' as barren still of everything but efforts to keep the peace somehow, since only so can he hope to keep his own weak head above water; and we see Octavius belatedly following Antony's politic advice to

> turn him off,
> Like to the empty ass, to shake his ears
> And graze in commons.

We meet Pompey, the foolish optimist, the lucky fighter cajoled to an unstable peace, standing on his honour, but as willing to profit by the vilest treachery. Ventidius is the one Roman to be found fighting Rome's enemies instead of his fellow Romans; and he dare not push victory home for fear of Antony's jealousy. We have Enobarbus; a man (the bitter paradox!) corrupted most by fidelity to his friend, then turning traitor—too late! Towards the play's end comes a very procession of generals, soldiers and dutiful servants, their fidelity abused, their valour wasted. Some desert while they can and some are caught in their leader's insensate ruin. While as to the Roman people themselves, the republic for which Brutus and Cassius died, the Friends, Romans, Countrymen who were Antony's 'good friends, sweet friends', what have their saviours and masters to say of them now? For Antony they are

> our slippery people,
>> Whose love is never linked to the deserver
>> Till his deserts are past . . .

and Cæsar, a scene or so later (it cannot be fortuitously), is made to speak of

> The ebb'd man, ne'er loved till ne'er worth love . . .

and, with what contempt, of how

>> This common body,
>> Like to a vagabond flag upon the stream,
>> Goes to and fro, lackeying the varying tide,
>> To rot itself with motion.

Not, on the whole then, a hopeful picture of the Roman world. And it is, in the main, Shakespeare's own picture; if he pillages Plutarch for facts, even for phrases, their

interpretation and emphasis—all that makes a picture—
are his.

Bradley will not place the play with the four great
tragedies, because, he says, Antony and Cleopatra themselves do not kindle pity and admiration to the full. He
admits, though, that their passion and its ending is by
no means the whole of the story. Certainly it is not.
What are we shown to begin with? Far less a pair of
tragic lovers in the making than—through the indignant
Roman eyes of Philo and Demetrius—a doting general,
effeminate in Egyptian finery,[3] ignoring Cæsar's messengers, capable of a

> Let Rome in Tiber melt, and the wide arch
> Of the ranged empire fall! . . .

(whoever will may hear it!), and a debauched Eastern
queen, mocking at things Roman, battening on his apos-
tasy. Here at once is the larger theme emphasized, the
discord which is to be resolved at last to a full close in
the elaborate confusions of their defeat and death.
The love-tragedy, we might almost say, is not made the
main question till no other question is left, till the
ruin wreaked by Triumvir and Queen is accomplished.
And the action of the play is schemed throughout for
the picturing of this wider ruin. Hence its diffuseness;
and hence, if this is not understood, much misunderstanding of its artistry.

'Feliciter audax,' says Coleridge of the style, and the
label has stuck. Dr. Johnson, however, is stern. 'The
events, of which the principal are described according
to history, are produced without any art of connection
or care of disposition.' It never does to neglect Johnson.
His plain-sailing sanity will cut a clear way for us
through many a metaphysical fog of nineteenth-century
criticism. Even if at last we must disagree with him, he

takes answering. But he owns besides that 'this play keeps curiosity always busy and the passions always interested' and that 'the continual hurry of the action, the variety of incidents, and the quick succession of one personage to another call the mind forward without intermission from the first Act to the last.' So in the end—Johnson exhibiting, perhaps, less consistency than usual—he and Coleridge are found not so far apart.

Feliciter audax! Shakespeare does seem to be amazingly at his ease. He brings in characters lavishly, flings Plutarch into dialogue; his verse is at its supplest, we are hardly conscious of the convention, and he shifts it to prose and back again without a jar. The action moves forthright and unchecked. Yet little or nothing in it shows superfluous; and, though endowed with but a line or two, the characters never fail to come to life. And if all this comes about 'without any art of connection or care of disposition', if it all seems haphazard, is it not just possible Shakespeare may mean it to, may at least be content that it should? There is little luck in these matters, as the inexpert playwright who tries his along these lines will find. Do we perhaps pay a tribute to this art in so condemning it? Critics have found themselves performing this feat before now. But, in fact, the play's scheme is plain and ordered enough once we grasp its purpose, and—the essential thing—once we relate it to the theatre of its nativity.

The Play's Construction

THE MAIN PROBLEM AND SOME MINOR ONES

WE should never, probably, think of Shakespeare as sitting down to construct a play as an architect must design a house, in the three dimensions of its building. His theatre did not call for this, as the more rigorous economics of modern staging may be said to do. He was liker to a musician, master of an instrument, who takes a theme and, by generally recognized rules, improvises on it; or even to an orator, so accomplished that he can carry a complex subject through a two-hour speech, split it up, run it by divers channels, digress, but never for too long, and at last bring the streams abreast again to blend them in his peroration. Clarity of statement, a sense of proportion, of the value of contrast, justness of emphasis—in these lie the technique involved; and these, it will be found, are the dominant qualities of Shakespeare's stagecraft—of the craft merely, be it understood.

He is apt to lay the main lines of his story very firmly and simply, and to let us see where we are going from the start, to cut the complexities from borrowed plots, and if any side issue later promises distraction, to make (literally) short work of it. Here he reduces the actual story to simplicity itself. Antony breaks from Cleopatra to patch up an insincere peace with Cæsar, since Pompey threatens them both; he marries Octavia, and deserts her to return to Cleopatra; war breaks out, Cæsar defeats them and they kill themselves. That is the plot; every character is concerned with it, hardly a line is spoken that does not relate to it; and much strength lies in this concentration of interest. There is no under-plot, nor any such obvious relief (which must, however, bring dissipation of interest too) as Falstaff, Nym, Bardolph, Pistol and Fluellen give to the heroics of the Henriad.

But, for a broad picturesque contrast, Roman and Egyptian are set against each other; and this opposition braces the whole body of the play, even as conflict between character and character will sustain each scene. He asserts the contrast at once; for we assemble expectant in a theatre, therefore first impressions cut deep and a first stretch of action will be of prime importance. We have the two indignant, hard-bitten Roman campaigners, who must stand aside while the procession passes—

Cleopatra, her ladies, the train, with Eunuchs fanning her.

—and see Antony in the toils. Their bitter comments follow it. Next, we have a taste of the chattering, shiftless, sensual, credulous Court, with its trulls and wizards and effeminates.[4] Then we see Antony, with Rome, the 'garboils' of his wife's making and the threats of Pompey calling him, breaking his toils for a time; and the statement of the theme is complete.

Do events now proceed (we ask Dr Johnson) 'without any art of connection or care of disposition'? We are shown Cæsar, the passionate Antony's passionless rival, correct and charmless, in conference with Lepidus—that third and very feeble pillar of the world!—upon their poor prospects, while Antony's 'lascivious wassails' hold him in Egypt. The action then swings back to a Cleopatra sighing after an Antony, who is already travelling Romeward; then to Pompey, questionably confident in his rising star.

> If the great gods be just, they shall assist
> The deeds of justest men.

Much virtue—and some risk—in such an if! And we pass at once to the knitting-up of the alliance that is to eclipse him.

Cæsar and Antony (when he is in his senses) are realists both, and there is neat wary work all round before their bargain is made, with the marriage to Octavia for a seal to it. A long passage, comparatively; but how artfully it is proportioned and modulated! First

comes the straight dispute between the rivals. This
must, of course, be given full importance, for here is
the play's main clash. But it is salted by the ironies
of Enobarbus, lightened by Lepidus and his fussi-
ness, eased by Mæcenas and Agricola and their tact.
Now, the dispute over and the alliance made, the worth
of it will be shown us. The great men depart to the
sound of trumpets; the three pillars of the world, mutual
in its support again. And while Antony, absent from our
sight, does his brisk wooing, Enobarbus talks to the
gloating Agrippa, and the somewhat shocked Mæcenas—
of Cleopatra! Note that the famous panegyric comes
from a coarse-mouthed cynic; he, too, can feel her
witchery.

> MÆCENAS. Now Antony must leave her utterly.
> ENOBARBUS. Never! He will not.
>   Age cannot wither her, nor custom stale
>   Her infinite variety. Other women cloy
>   The appetites they feed: but she makes hungry
>   Where most she satisfies; for vilest things
>   Become themselves in her, that the holy priests
>   Bless her when she is riggish.

With this in our ears,

> *Enter Antony, Cæsar, Octavia between them.*

and we hear Octavia (the difference!) with her gentle
gravity, saying

> Before the gods my knee shall bow my prayers
> To them for you.

So Shakespeare weaves his pattern—for another
simile—as he goes along, setting colour against colour,
coarse thread by fine. And certainly the thing is done
with such seeming ease and natural subtlety that we

hardly note the artistry involved. We should feel the flat
poverty of its absence soon enough.

Now another thread is woven in. The Soothsayer,
symbol of the East, comes shadowing Antony, warping
and weakening his will.[5] Then follows (contrast again) a
touch of Roman energy; Ventidius is dispatched to Parthia. Then we are flung back to Egypt and to Cleopatra;
and in redoubled contrast—for Shakespeare has now
begun to bite upon the ironies of his theme—to a
Cleopatra most unlike the golden vision of Cydnus, a
spitting fury that hales the messenger of Antony's faith-
lessness up and down by the hair of his head. Truly

> Age cannot wither her, nor custom stale
> Her infinite variety.

Now we return to Cæsar and his policies, to the successful manoeuvring of Pompey to a peace, thanks to Antony
and his prestige. What the worth of this also will be we
learn as before when the great men have done and their
followers talk things over (harsh truths are heard in ante-
rooms). Or we might judge it for ourselves by its crowning
in a drinking bout. The wretched Lepidus cannot last this
out; and that first bitter outbreak at the sight of the
'strumpet's fool' has its derisive echo in Enobarbus'

> There's a strong fellow, Menas. . . . 'A bears the third part of
> the world, man: see'st not?

And the chivalrous Pompey, we find, would be glad to
have his guests' throats cut—by someone less chivalrous
than he! Cæsar alone keeps his head; but we hardly like
him the better for that. Then, sharp upon the crapulous
business, Shakespeare shows us

> *Ventidius, as it were in triumph, . . the dead body of Pacorus borne
> before him.*

He has beaten back the Parthians. But now he dare not,
for his own safety's sake, do Rome better service still,
with such masters—hers and his—jealously watching
him.

> Oh Silius, Silius,
> I have done enough; a lower place, note well,
> May make too great an act: for learn this, Silius;
> Better to leave undone, than by our deed
> Acquire too high a fame when him we serve's away.

Here is so notable and typical a piece of stagecraft
that it is worth while to try and see the full effect of it.
There is, of course, the aspect, which any alert reader
discovers: the contrasting of the soldiers at their duty
with the rulers at their drinking bout.[6] But we must keep
Shakespeare's stage well in mind if we are to realize the
dramatic value to the spectator of the quick shift from
singing and dancing and the confusion of tipsy embrac-
ings to the strict military march that brings Ventidius *as
in triumph* upon the stage. There was no pause at all;
Enobarbus and Menas would hardly have vanished, their
drunken halloos would still be echoing when Ventidius
and his procession appeared. This set the contrast at its
sharpest; yet, since change of scene did not mean change
of scenery, there was no distracting of mind or eye, a
unity of effect was kept, and the action flowed on
unchecked.

With one more interweaving of themes we shall be
halfway through the play. Enobarbus' and Agrippa's
mockeries give an acrid aftertaste to feast, treaty and
marriage, all three; and we are to guess that poor
Lepidus—so spendthrift of good nature!—will be made
bankrupt soon. Antony and Octavia take their loving
farewell of Cæsar and lovingly depart. An instant after
we see Cleopatra, recovered from her fury, having

Octavia's attractions picked to pieces for her comfort by the much repentant messenger.

> Dull of tongue and dwarfish! . . .
> Widow! Charmian, hark! . . .
>   Why, methinks by him
> This creature's no such thing. . . .
> The man hath seen some majesty, and should know. . . .
> All may be well enough.

And, watching her smile, we need have little doubt but that it will be. Very little; for as she leaves the stage (yet again only upon an Elizabethan stage will the effect fully count),

Enter Antony and Octavia.

with the rift that is to part them already showing.

Thus (if Johnson still needs answering, we can turn his own words against him now) curiosity has been kept busy and the passions interested, and the continual hurry of the action, the variety of incidents and the quick succession of one personage to another have called the mind forward without intermission . . . which is what Shakespeare has set out to do. He has told his story, woven his pattern, kept conflict alive and balance true, character prompting action, and action elucidating character, neither made to halt for the other. This really is the be-all and end-all of his stagecraft—and might well be said to be of any stagecraft; it is only the application of the method that will differ from stage to stage.

We may note in passing how he turns one small technical difficulty that he stumbles on to his profit (he has always had the faculty of doing this), and thereafter how he cuts his way out of another. Throughout this first part of the play he has more Roman than Egyptian material to deal with. Somehow he must keep the balance true and Cleopatra pretty constantly in our minds; but all the story asks is that she should be left by Antony and then sit waiting, patiently or impatiently, for his return. A more mechanical minded playwright would have begun, then, with Cæsar and Pompey, and so have accounted for some of the overplus at once; would have made, consequently, a mild beginning, and given a minor interest precedence. With Shakespeare what most matters will have pride of place, nor will he, when he has it, abate a chance; and, as we see, he lets the impulse of his opening carry him to the point of Antony's departure, over a stretch of 365 lines, abundant in life and colour (it is actually a tenth of the entire play), till he has his story's master-motive made fertile in our minds. But now he must eke out the rest of the Egyptian material very carefully. The glimpse of Cleopatra pursuing her Antony before he is well away from her with 'twenty several messengers' could (if the need were rather for compression) be dispensed with; but it is true and significant Cleopatra, so this may fill up a space. What next? When the news of her lover's treachery has been brought her the material will have run out; so this episode is split up and spread over two scenes. And at once Shakespeare sees and seizes the chance to show us, first the savage and suffering Cleopatra; next, on the rebound, the colder, baser-na-tured woman, feeding on flattery and deceit—and well aware of their worth. The story is moulded to the development of character. Each scene of Cleopatra's, throughout this first part of the play, adds something to our knowledge of her; they accumulate to inform the tragedy of her end.

But now, though the two themes are abreast (Antony's concord with Cæsar seen on the wane, while Cleopatra, spiderlike, sits spinning a new web for him), it is clear, both that the Roman political material still outmeasures the Egyptian and that it may lengthen this part of the play into dangerous monotony. The Antony-Octavia theme might be elaborated for a variation. Shakespeare decides against this; it would still leave Cleopatra in the air. There is no more for her to do, that's evident, till Antony returns to her. Roman politics, then, must in turn suffer heroic compression. The wars upon Pompey and his murder, Cæsar's new quarrel with Antony, the extinction of Lepidus, are reported in a scene or so.

But neither are we shown Antony's return to Cleopatra; Cæsar recounts it to Octavia and his friends. There were other reasons against this. Shakespeare is not, as we have argued, writing a mere love-story, he is transplanting history to the stage; the causes and circumstances of the quarrel and the war that is to end at Actium are, at this juncture, the more important matter to him, and they must be given the widest significance words can give them, a wider if vaguer significance than concrete action will give. He could have shown us effectively enough how

> In Alexandria . . .
> I' the market-place, on a tribunal silvered,
> Cleopatra and himself [Antony] in chairs of gold
> Were publicly enthroned. . . .

But in Cæsar's

> No, my most wronged sister, Cleopatra
> Hath nodded him to her. He hath given his Empire
> Up to a whore; who now are levying
> The kings o' the earth for war. He hath assembled
> Bocchus, the king of Libya; Archelaus,
> Of Cappadocia; Philadelphos, king
> Of Paphlagonia; the Thracian king, Adallas;

> King Manchus of Arabia; King of Pont;
> Herod of Jewry; Mithridates, king
> Of Comagene; Polemon and Amyntas,
> The kings of Mede and Lycaonia,
> With a more larger list of sceptres.

a threat to the whole Roman world seems sounded.

Besides, the play's crisis is to come. These scenes are preparation for it, no more; they must be kept tense, but low in tone. The rivals are still only strengthening themselves for the struggle, with indignation as with arms.

Incidentally, Shakespeare will be glad to avoid a scene of reconciliation if it is to involve his boy-actress in any sort of 'amorous transports'. The play is dominated by sexual passion, no bones are made about the carnality of it either; yet how carefully he avoids writing any scene which a boy could not act without unpleasantness or in fear of ridicule![7] The fatal reunion is far more significantly marked by Cleopatra's spitfire quarrel with Enobarbus.

> CLEOPATRA. I will be even with thee, doubt it not . . .
>   Thou hast forspoke my being in these wars,
>   And sayst it is not fit.
> ENOBARBUS. Well, is it, is it? . . .
>   Your presence needs must puzzle Antony,
>   Take from his heart, take from his brain, from's time,
>   What should not then be spared. He is already
>   Traduced for levity, and 'tis said in Rome,
>   That Photinus an Eunuch, and your maids
>   Manage this war.

For from this it is that disaster springs; this is the beginning of the end.

Yet we are but halfway through the play; and here is another sign that a larger theme than the love-story is being worked out. Would Shakespeare otherwise be giving, against all precedent, half his play's length to its catastrophe? Now, it is the craft and the art of this long ending that have been most distorted by editors, its intention most grievously misunderstood by critics. A producer must not only start afresh from the untouched text, he must read it in the light of a clear understanding of the stage of its origin.[8]

The Question of Act-Division

To begin with he must free the play from act and scene divisions. The Folio gives none. The first five-act division was Rowe's. Johnson thought the first scene of his second act might better be the last scene of his first, but added ' . . . it is of small importance, where these unconnected and desultory scenes are interrupted.' Pope made the first scene of Rowe's fifth act into the last scene of Act IV, and after this all the later editors seem to have fallen unquestioningly into line. A five-act division for any play has, of course, its sanctions. The editors of the Folio indulge in it when they think they will. They (they or their printer for them) start out each time with an *Actus Primus, Scæna Prima*; a schoolboy's heading for his copybook. Sometimes they keep this up, once or twice they get halfway through the play and give it up; sometimes, as with *Antony and Cleopatra*, they just leave it at that. Now, whatever other dramatists may have done, whatever Shakespeare may have done in other plays, whatever may have been the custom of the public and private theatres for which he wrote—and it was probably a differing and a changing one—in the matter of making pauses during a performance, and whether those pauses were formal or prolonged, in this play there is no *dramatically* indicated act-division at all. There is, that is to say, (as far as I can discover) no juncture where the play's acting will be made more effective by a pause. On the contrary, each scene has an effective relation to the next, which a pause between them will weaken or destroy. There may have been four pauses in the original performing, or three, two or one; there may have been none at all, though that is hardly likely. But it would always (again, as far as I can discern) be a question of custom or convenience, not of dramatic effect.

Granted five acts, a case can be made for Rowe's choice of them, or Johnson's, or Pope's, or for half a dozen others, doubtless; and as good a one perhaps for a four-act division or a three. And if, pleading weakness of the flesh in actors or audience, a producer thinks it well to split the play into two, he can call a convenient halt, he'll find, at the turn of the action when Antony's drift back to Cleopatra is plainly to be seen. He may pause with some effect after that

> All may be well enough.

or pass on a little further before he pauses and begins again (perhaps with better) with the news that

> Cæsar and Lepidus have made wars upon Pompey.

or with Cæsar's own outburst of indignation and the return of Octavia; or, more forcibly still, with the squabble between Cleopatra and Enobarbus and the launching of the war. But let him plead convenience merely; for any halt hereabouts must mean rather the loss of an effect than the making one. And this will be as true of any other pauses in any other places; and the lengthier they are the worse it will be.

For the fact is that Shakespeare's work never parcels up very well. He was not among those writers who industriously gather material, sort and arrange and rearrange it before they fit it together. When his mood is operative he creates out of an abundance of vitality, and it is no good service to him to start obstructing the flow of it. He keeps, however, for all his fervour, a keen sense of form; it is largely in this marriage of impulse and control that his genius as pure playwright lies. And when inspiration flags, he must come to contriving. He is businesslike at that, quite callously businesslike sometimes. But even to the most workaday stuff he gives a certain force. And should carelessness—for he can be wickedly careless—land him in a tight place, there is, to the practiced observer, a sort of sporting interest in seeing him so nimbly and recklessly get out of it.

He does not (*pace* Dr Johnson) write haphazardly; it is not that. He plans—and more spaciously than those that have need to plan. He is seldom to be found following a formula, even a proved one of his own. Incidental devices he'll use again and again, as we all repeat words and phrases—and the deeper (one notices) the feelings beneath them the simpler these are apt to be. He is the last man we should look to find submitting himself to an arbitrary scheme, whatever its sanction, a five-act scheme or any other. Custom might even be imposing this on a play's performance and impose it no further on him. And by now he has brought much to the theatre, broken much new ground, has the medium very plastic in his hands. With such a task as this before him, and his imagination fired, he will be out to do it as effectively as he can. There will be no other question. He will have to muster all his resources, and he will need full freedom for the use of them.

A Digression, Mainly upon the Meaning of the Word 'Scene'

BUT it is hard for us to meet him with a mind as free. The medium that he worked in so spontaneously is alien to us. Even the nomenclature under which we discuss it betrays us to error. Setting disputable act-division aside, what do we mean by scene-division and by 'scene'? There are no reliable scene-divisions in the Quartos.[9] The editors of the Folio sometimes run to them, and they customarily draw their dividing lines at each clearance of the stage. But this does not commit them to an imagined change of place, nor connote any check to the action.[10] By Rowe's time, however, 'scene' had taken on, though still uncertainly, a new meaning. Painted scenery, of a more or less conventional sort, was in current use. This defined locality; and a change of scene meant a change of place, was a diversion and a check to the action in every sense. The old fluidity of the Elizabethan stage, which really could 'call the mind forward without intermission', was gone.

If Rowe finds act-division in the Folio he leaves it, and he cuts the plays with none to a similar pattern. His chief editorial task is to give them geography; but as he leaves scene-division too when he finds it he cannot do this very consistently; his 'scene' being no longer the 'scene' of the Folio editors. In *As You Like It*, for instance, he must leave some of the old scene-divisions unexplained; there are far too many for him. In *Othello* there are too few; the action will not abide throughout some of these where he has placed it. In *A Midsummer Night's Dream* he announces, to begin with, *Athens, and a wood not far from it*, and troubles no more. He looks at the plays when he can in the light of his own theatre, for he is presenting them to readers accustomed to it. He

48

disregards the many signs that they do not really belong there; the matter, for one thing, is of no great importance, for another, some memory of the old theatre still survives.

Antony and Cleopatra, however, offers Rowe a clean sheet, and he takes trouble. At first he does no more scene-dividing than the sense of place in his own stagecraft compels him to. He is content with a generalized *Alexandria; Rome; Sicily; The coast of Italy near Misenum; Athens.* He particularizes the very obvious *Pompey's Galley*, and later rises to the enthusiasm of *A Magnificent Monument.* But the comings and goings of the three days' battle defeat him. *Cæsar's camp* is a clear enough locality. *Cleopatra's Palace* and *Before the walls of Alexandria* will do. But the manoeuvrings of the armies, and, above all, that tiresome *noise of a sea-fight*, cannot be given exact place; and he is still free enough from realism to let them, with a few more such confusions, take their chance. Nevertheless he has now turned the long, unchecked stretch of action which was Shakespeare's into an Act III and IV of eight localized scenes each.[11] Later editors are to better him. As the theatre of their day moves ever further from Elizabethan freedom and is the more committed to integrity of place they, for their part, dissect and define ever more closely; till modern editions give us a third act of thirteen scenes and a fourth of fifteen, with *A Plain near Actium; Another part of the Plain; Another part of the Plain*, following each other breathlessly. Only that tiresome *noise of a sea-fight* still refuses its pigeonhole.

What of Shakespeare's stagecraft is left? What dramatic purpose of any kind is conveyed by this?

Act III. *Scene viii. A plain near Actium.*

Enter Cæsar and Taurus with his army, marching.

CÆSAR. Taurus!

TAURUS. My lord?

CÆSAR. Strike not by land; keep whole: provoke not battle
Till we have done at sea. Do not exceed
The prescript of this scroll: our fortune lies
Upon this jump.

Exeunt.

Scene ix. Another part of the Plain.
Enter Antony and Enobarbus.

ANTONY. Set we our squadrons on yond' side o' the hill,
In eye of Cæsar's battle; from which place
We may the number of the ships behold,
And so proceed accordingly.

Exeunt.

Scene x. Another part of the Plain.
Canidius marcheth with his land army one way over the stage; and
Taurus, the lieutenant of Cæsar, the other way. After their going in is
heard the noise of a sea-fight.
Alarum. Enter Enobarbus.

ENOBARBUS. Naught, naught, all naught! I can behold no longer:
Th' Antoniad, the Egyptian admiral,
With all their sixty, fly and turn the rudder. . . .

This last so-called 'scene' does run on for thirty-five lines
more.

The layman must remember that he is reading a play,
and should be imaginatively translating it into performance as he reads. Into what sort of performance do
the editors help him to translate this, and the whole
stretch of action from the eve of the first battle with
Cæsar to the carrying of Antony dying to the Monument? They parcel it into twenty-two scenes, two of four

lines each, one of six, one of nine, one of ten, three of
sixteen lines and two of twenty-two; the rest are of more
normal length. Scenes, as the editors of the Folio understood the word, they may be; as localized scenes they
make dramatic nonsense.

Do the modern editors mean us to envisage the play
in performance with painted scenery shifting every
minute or so, transporting us round Actium, from one
camp to another, to Alexandria and back again? Apparently. They know that Shakespeare's theatre provided for
nothing of the sort; do they never stop to think what the
effect of this cinematographic patchwork of their devising
must be?[12] But strike out their place-headings, and still
think in terms of 'scenes', and even then where are we?
For Sir Edmund Chambers, who carries the Elizabethan
stage pretty vividly in his eye, can tell us that in these
passages 'Shakespeare is in some danger of outrunning
the apprehensions of his auditory.'

Is it so? Sir Edmund will be using the word 'auditory'
with intention; but is he thinking of its members, not as
listening merely, and looking at the actors, but imaginatively staring beyond them, making efforts to conjure
up backgrounds that are never described, barely indicated, and being kept on the jump, asking themselves—
while Cæsar and his men leave the stage empty for
Antony and his men to fill it, only to leave it in a
moment to Cæsar again—'Where on earth are we now?'

If the play's first audiences sat trying to do anything
of the sort, Shakespeare certainly did outrun their apprehensions; and if Sir Edmund supposes that Shakespeare meant them to, no wonder he is dubious about its
stagecraft; and no wonder that critics with not a tithe of
his knowledge, vaguely agreeing, will cry it down. But
(with respect) Shakespeare's intentions were utterly different, and his audiences were not puzzled at all.

Convention in art is hard to discount, and we accept the accustomed conventions of the theatre more unquestioningly than most. The visual side of our modern 'realistic' drama is itself conventional; but it has come, by slow degrees, so fully to its own that we are apt to apply the laws of it, quite unconsciously, to every sort of theatre and play, as if they were natural laws.[13] The 'visual law' of drama was, to the Elizabethans, a very different, and an arbitrary and inconstant thing besides. It had existed, crudely, in the miracle plays, and it became elaborately, decoratively dominant in the Masques. But on the public stages it was, for various reasons, unprofitably hard to develop, and only in the candle-lit 'private' theatres were its claims finally made good. By 'visual law' must be understood, of course, not the sight of the actors and their acting, unescapable in any play, but their environment, the background, against which they show, and which can be as histrionic in its kind as they. We are now so used to seeing this pictured, be it as *A drawing room in Mayfair*, or as *Piccadilly Circus*, or *The Forest of Arden*, or *A street in Venice*, or *Verona*, or *Rome*, that if it is not set before us we set ourselves to imagine it there; and we assume that the Elizabethans did the same—for, after all, the characters in a play must be somewhere. Yes, they must be, if we push the inquiry. But the Elizabethan dramatist seldom encourages us to push it; and his first audiences assuredly, as a rule, did not do so in despite of him. For them the actors were very plainly on the stage, but the characters might, half the time, be nowhere in particular. It was, for the dramatist of that day, a privilege akin to the novelist's, who may, if he chooses, detach characters, through page after page, from fixed surroundings. It was a freedom which the promise of the scenic stage gradually sapped; but Shakespeare, at least, never surrendered it, and we here find him in the maturity of his craftsmanship, enjoying and exploiting it to the full.

He will always have, of course, as the novelist has, the whereabouts of his characters in mind, and casual allusion to it will crop out. There may also be the demands of the action for a house door, a balcony, a tree or a cavern to be satisfied; but these things will have rather the utility of furniture than the value of scenery. And—this is the point—he need never give more attention to his play's background than he feels will be dramatically profitable. Moreover, he can give it—yet again as does the novelist—the *sort* of attention he chooses. Look at *Richard II*. Poetry is lavished on the characters and the theme in general. But it is never put to use for the verbal painting of a background.

> Believe me, noble lord,
> I am a stranger here in Gloucestershire:
> These high wild hills and rough uneven ways
> Draw out our miles and make them wearisome.

is the extremest instance of it. We are left, as a rule, to judge by the tenor of the action where the actors are; and in many cases it would be impossible for the listener to say. If we need to know with any precision, the simple label of such a line as

> Barkloughly Castle call they this at hand?

will suffice to tell us.

Take two of the Comedies.

> Well, this is the Forest of Arden.

sets us (in *As You Like It*) accurately enough where Shakespeare wishes us to be.[14] Scene after scene, so called, once this impression is given us, may be taking place anywhere thereabouts; and, as it is a comedy of character, not much time is spent upon picturing the forest itself. Such description of it as we do get is fantastic and reflects the artifice of the story. But *A Midsummer Night's Dream* is one long lyrical painting of the wood near Athens, with its English banks of primroses and thyme, the oxlip and the nodding violet; for this is what the play's theme demands.

From such direct simplicity as this turn to *Macbeth*, to such passages as

> This castle hath a pleasant seat; the air
> Nimbly and sweetly recommends itself
> Unto our gentle senses. . . .

as

> The west yet glimmers with some streaks of day;
> Now spurs the lated traveller apace
> To gain the timely inn. . . .

to the recurring chorus of the witches—the play's writing is full of pictorial suggestion. It is suggestion rather than description, an elaborate creating of atmosphere:

> Light thickens; and the crow
> Makes wing to the rooky wood. . . .

Description in this play is, indeed, as nothing compared with suggestion. Whereabouts in the castle at Inverness we are throughout the comings and goings of Duncan's tragic sojourn we should never know if the editors did not tell us, nor what the rooms or courtyards look like. But what scene-painter will create such darkness for us as that in which a magic of words wraps the night of the murder?

But all through, and in every phase of Shakespeare's development, it is a question of dramatic profit and the particular need of the play. In *Antony and Cleopatra* we find, except for the one episode of the sentries on guard listening to the mysterious music, no verbal scene-painting of any sort, direct or implicit, nor, as we have noted, more than the very minimum of reference to the locality of the scenes. The reason is plain. It is a play of action and of multiplied incident. The story is simple, but the tributary threads of it are manifold, and the interweaving conflicts of purpose complex enough. Its theme (once again) is not merely Antony's love for Cleopatra, but his ruin as general and statesman, the final ascension of Octavius, and the true end of

> that work the ides of March begun.

Therefore the dead Fulvia's doings, Pompey's grievances, Cæsar's policy, Lepidus and his timeserving, Ventidius balked of a bigger victory—these things and their like are of first importance, and we must be kept alive to them. But an audience has only a certain amount of attention to bestow, and it must be economized. It does not matter much where Cæsar and Lepidus, Pompey and Menecrates and Menas have their talks, nor whether the bargaining with Antony takes place indoors or out; so Shakespeare spends hardly a thought or a line upon it. Nor upon the beauties of the prospect—nor the weather! Antony and Cæsar, we feel, would certainly take a prosaic view of such things; and, for our part, we shall know them no better for viewing them against a picturesque background. But that each turn in the battle of their quick, ruthless Roman minds should be made clear to us—this matters a great deal, and to this all else, if need be, is sacrificed. Emotion, and at full pitch, is in store; but it will not be freed till the issues of the action are narrowing to the point of solution. Meanwhile, we have clarity, the clarity of a desert landscape, the theme in its stark integrity. *Antony and Cleopatra* is, among other things, the most businesslike of plays.

And if, for a beginning, this has been Shakespeare's aim, how much more, when we come to the confusions of the three days' battle, with its blunders and false hopes, its chances and changes, must not perfect clarity be achieved? Nor in the writing only, and by suppressing picturesque inessentials. Could he do what he sets out to do if he did not now exploit to the full the freedom from circumstance which the convention of his stage allows him? For this in itself gives clarity; it lets the dramatist concentrate upon the single subject. Complicate these twenty-two 'scenes' as they flash past us by thinking of their whereabouts, and our limited power of attention will certainly not suffice.[15] But listen without further conjecture to the mere tale as the dialogue unfolds it, and watch just what we are asked to watch, the characters as they come and go and the symbolic marching of the armies, and there is no confusion whatever—only such, at any rate, as Shakespeare is at positive pains to be painting for us, in the hectic uncertainties through which Antony moves to his end.

An audience need do no more than listen and look at what there is to see and ask no questions. And audiences, as a fact, do no more than they are asked to do. Would that they always did that! Nothing will be heard of Actium, nor of a plain near it, nor anything of the sort. There is talk of the obviously distant Toryne and Peloponnesos. But from the beginning of this long stretch of action to the end, till Antony is carried dying to the Monument, there is hardly a hint to let us know where, at any moment, we may imaginatively be. Shakespeare does not set out to inform us, and he might sometimes be hard put to it to say himself.

Cæsar sits down in Alexandria. . . .

we are told. The next day he is to be beaten to his camp, and Antony will give the order:

Through Alexandria make a jolly march.

But that same night, with Cæsar still in occupation, Antony's sentries are on guard 'about the streets'. What streets? What does it matter? Just nothing at all. We not only do not want to know; it would be worse than useless to trouble us with the information.

If Shakespeare knows these things himself (perhaps he does) and wants to tell us, there are half a dozen ways open. He never seems to have rejected simplicities of the

Barkloughly Castle call they this at hand?

sort merely because they were simple. He can range from this to the subtle expounding of geography and history, too, by which Ventidius lets us know where he is in the first few lines spoken upon his entrance *as in triumph*. But, simply done or subtly, this sort of thing would over-lengthen the action here, check its flow and distract our attention—as badly, almost, as our own perverse efforts to imagine a whereabouts for each 'scene' distract it.

To give anything of the spaciousness of a true scene to the four or five terse lines, by which now Cæsar, now Antony, show us the quality of their generalship, they would need to be multiplied by four; and this would weaken the present effect even in magnifying it. The larger episodes could easily be localized; but the others would then lose substance by comparison; what is more, the unity of the whole complex event would be de-stroyed. And it is in this unity that its dramatic strength lies. It is by the welding of the mixed mass of incident and character into a consistent whole, freed from all irrelevant circumstance, that its value is isolated and made clear. Obliterate scenic locality, we have still the stage itself left, with its formal furnishings, certainly. But make-believe makes short work of those familiar features; and, once we are enthralled and they vanish, there is nothing left to stand between us and the essential drama; we are at one with its realities. Here, surely, is a technical achievement of some account.

Why show us this long panorama of detail? Why not (as a Greek and probably a modern dramatist would) plan a few full-charged organic, significant scenes, and shape and compress the story to fit them? Again (if we could imagine Shakespeare putting himself the question) the answer is plain. Antony's is a great captain's downfall, the end of a man who has ruled half the Roman world, and we are to see both why he ends and how; and to see, as near as may be, the very process of it. The poor strategy, the weak will, the useless bargaining, set against Cæsar's steady mind; these are as significant every whit as the passion that wreaks vengeance on the wretched Thidias[16] and storms at Cleopatra. And the strung-out sequence of events, that are tense often and feverish while they matter little, slackened to triteness though they matter much, now catching up, now shedding their actors as they pass, time and place apt to seem the most fortuitous things about them—does not this both show us the true process of the matter, and give us, besides, just the impression that in life will belong to our share in such a crisis? Bouts of noisy fighting with heart-rent love-scenes in between would doubtless make a good show. But here, if Plutarch tells true, is a picture of the business of war as these Roman realists waged it, with luck and cunning, passion and judgement and interest all at odds in leaders and followers too. It is history directly dramatized.

Shakespeare neither takes nor uses his material haphazardly. If, with one dramatic aim, he frees himself from ties of place, with another he creates for himself ties of time. He telescopes Plutarch's vague weeks into a strict three days. They mark the ebb and flow and ebb of Antony's fortunes. First, there is the night's carouse after defeat, while the sentries keep their strange watch; then the next night's after victory, while Cæsar's sentries mark Enobarbus creeping out to die; then the third day's ebb to disaster. This gives him rhythm and form, and increases tension; it makes the story clearer, and our interest easier to hold. It is deliberate stagecraft.

The Play's Construction, *Continued*

THE THREE DAYS' BATTLE

WE are plunged, for a beginning to the business, amid the squabbling distractions of Antony's counsels. Enobarbus, level-headed, caustic of tongue, does what he can to stem the tide of folly. Antony stands, weakly obstinate, under Cleopatra's eye. Against all reason, he will meet the enemy at sea—

> For that he dares us to't.

The news accumulates of Cæsar's swift, unchecked advance. We have the veteran legionary breaking all bounds of discipline in a last desperate protest.

> O noble emperor, do not fight by sea;
> Trust not to rotten planks: do you misdoubt
> This sword, and these my wounds?

Then, as they disappear,

> *Enter Cæsar, with his army, marching.*

The first day's fighting is compressed into the symbolism (it is little more) of a dozen lines of dialogue and business. This is a sort of variation upon the old dumb show, to an Elizabethan audience a familiar and pregnant convention. But note the niceties of effect. Cæsar enters *with his army, marching*; a formal processional entrance, capping the news of his approach that has threaded the preceding scene. In two sentences he shows us his strategy and his quality in command. Next, Antony and Enobarbus appear alone on the emptied stage. Antony speaks four hurried and half-purposed lines, Enobarbus never a word, but his glum looks will be eloquent; and they vanish. Then comes the marching and countermarching of the armies that are not to fight (pure symbolism!), each with its subordinate general in command. The stage empties again, and its emptiness holds us expectant. Then, of a sudden, comes the climax, the significant event; *the noise of a sea-fight* is heard.[17] Then, actual drama reasserting itself, Enobarbus, with alarums to reinforce his fury, bursts upon us, tongue-tied no more, to interpret disaster with

> Naught, naught, all naught! I can behold no longer:
> Th' Antoniad, the Egyptian admiral,
> With all their sixty, fly and turn the rudder. . . .

He is reinforced by Scarus, younger and fierier still[18]:

>   Gods and goddesses,
>   All the whole synod of them! . . .
>   The greater cantle of the world is lost
>   With very ignorance; we have kissed away
>   Kingdoms and provinces.

This symbolism of war is not in itself dramatic, one sees. Shakespeare could hardly make it so, but he hardly needs it to be. He gives us, however, very little of it. His drama lies in the consequences of the fighting, as these are reflected in the conduct of his characters. We are shown, it is to be remarked, no actual fighting at all, come no nearer to it than the sight of young Scarus and his fresh wounds. He is marked out for us as the gallant warrior, and Antony gives him generous praise. Antony's own valour we may take for granted. But his challenge to Cæsar to fight him single-handed is stressed, and as a ridiculous thing. Says Enobarbus:

> Cæsar, thou hast subdued
> His judgment too.

This is stressed because in it and all it implies lie his failure and his tragedy.

The sequel to the first battle is shown us at length. Scarus' boyish wrath spends itself; Enobarbus, shame rankling deeper in him, relapses to his gibing; Canidius coolly plans to make his peace with Cæsar, and departs, no man hindering him; Antony appears. The gradation from the convention of the battle to the actuality of the scene to come between the broken Antony and Cleopatra, all repentance, is nicely adjusted. First we have had the angry agony of defeat, which needs human expression; next, the few lines Canidius speaks give us an abstract of many happenings; then Antony, in the exhaustion of despair, sums up against himself and tells to the end the chapter of disaster. Here is Plutarch's ' . . . and so Antonius . . . went and sat down alone in the prowe of his ship, and said never a word, clapping his head between both his hands . . . and so lived three days alone without speaking to any man. But when he arrived at the head of Tænarus there Cleopatra's women first brought Antonius and Cleopatra to speak together, and afterwards to sup and lie together. . . . Now for himself he determined to crosse over into Africk and toke one

of his carects or hulks loden with gold and silver and
other rich cariage, and gave it unto his friends, com-
manding them to depart, and to seeke to save themselves. They answered him weeping, that they would
nether doe it nor yet forsake him. Then Antonius very
curteously and lovingly did comfort them. . . . ' And it is
interesting to see how Shakespeare, contracting the circumstances, can yet keep the sense and temper of the
events, can even, by the tune and rhythm of a dozen
lines of verse, by a suggestive phrase or so, and by the
indicated business of the scene, give us the slack sense
of days of breathing-space following on the blow.

The encounter with Cleopatra brings us back to matter
more his own, and of more immediacy, closer therefore in
tension. It is to be the first of three in which Antony will
face perforce the truth of what is between them, mounting
the scale of suffering to madness at the last. This one, then,
must be in a low key (Shakespeare even skirts the edge of
the comic at its start, with the leading of Cleopatra,
spectacularly pitiful, up to the weeping hero), and it holds
no contest; he is but too ready with his

> Fall not a tear, I say; one of them rates
> All that is won and lost. . . .

We pass to Cæsar's diplomatic exploiting of his victory,
his curt rejection of Antony's overtures, the sending of
Thidias to wean Cleopatra from him. Antony rises to
nobility again, with his 'Let her know't' for sole comment
upon the offer of peace to Cleopatra if she will yield
him up. But with his next breath he falls to the fatuity
of the challenge to Cæsar.

There follows Cleopatra's ignoble reception of Thidias.
Enobarbus can have at least one taste of revenge upon
her, and Antony is fetched to see her smiling on Cæsar's
messenger.

> 'Tis better playing with a lion's whelp
> Than with an old one dying.

The savage outburst, which sends the glib fellow back, dumb and bleeding from his stripes, is, for all its passion, as futile—and is meant to seem so—as were the heroics of the challenge; so is the moral stripping and lashing of Cleopatra. For, his rage glutted and appeased by the sight of the wretch half-slaughtered at his feet, he can turn back to her, open-eyed to the truth about her, and, listening to the easy lies, can end them with an easier—and a hopeless—

> I am satisfied.

After this we may be sure that he is doomed. Enobarbus is sure of it, and Cæsar's comment is contemptuous and brief. Shakespeare adds, for the ending of the day, the strange little hysterical passage in which, by

> one of those odd tricks which sorrow shoots
> Out of the mind...

we find him melting his followers to tears as he pathetically paints the prospects of his defeat and death—to show us yet again, one supposes, how helplessly off the rails the man has run.[19]

Now comes, to mark the passing of the night, the episode of the sentries on their watch. It is, as we have noted, the one piece of scene-painting in the play; a developing of atmosphere, rather—for the single line,

> Heard you of nothing strange about the streets?

is the only hint of locality—of the ominous atmosphere of a night of reprieve between battles. The means to it are merely a few whispering voices and the

> *Music of the hoboyes ... under the stage.*

It is after the couples have met, gossiped a moment and parted with 'good-night,' that they hear this.

4TH SOLDIER.   Peace! what noise?
IST SOLDIER.   List, list!
2ND SOLDIER.   Hark!
IST SOLDIER.   Music i' the air!
3RD SOLDIER.   Under the earth.
4TH SOLDIER.   It signs well, does it not?
3RD SOLDIER.   No.
IST SOLDIER.   Peace, I say.
              What should this mean?
2ND SOLDIER.   'Tis the god Hercules, whom Antony loved,
              Now leaves him.

They feel their way towards each other and whisper confusedly in the darkness, their nerves a little ragged.

2ND SOLDIER. How now, masters!
ALL TOGETHER.   How now?
        How now? do you hear this?
IST SOLDIER.   Ay: is't not strange?
3RD SOLDIER. Do you hear, masters? do you hear?
IST SOLDIER. Follow the noise so far as we have quarter.
           Let's see how it will give off.
      ALL.   Content! 'Tis strange.

And, holding all together as the music dies into distance, they vanish. The entire effect, simple in itself, is made with masterly economy. The scene has two uses: it preserves the continuity of the action, and is gloom before the bright beginning of the second day.

Antony has not slept. He comes jovial and confident from night-long revelry, calling for his squire. Cleopatra, seeming a lissom girl again, beneath the spell of this still magnificent spendthrift of fortune, plays at buckling on his armour; and with shouts and the flourish of trumpets and the clangour of the gathering of armed men Shakespeare rings up the dawn. Trumpets sound again; it is as if they set out to sure victory. Two notes of doubt are struck: by a shrewder Cleopatra with her

> That he and Cæsar might
> Determine this great war in single fight!
> Then, Antony—! But now—?

—before she retires to her chamber to recover what she may of her lost night's rest; and by the news, greeting Antony as he marches forth, that Enobarbus—Enobarbus!—has deserted. He puts the treason behind him with a gentle magnanimity which comes strangely—does it?—from a man who could have his enemy's ambassador half flayed alive. But this is Antony.

Next we see Cæsar. But this—upon a mere half-victory won—is an overconfident Cæsar, not the cautious general of the earlier battle. Between the brilliant opening and the brilliant end of Antony's day we have, for contrast, Enobarbus repentant. There is, of course, no strict measuring out of time; and we return to some degree of symbolism when, after alarum, drums and trumpets, Agrippa enters with

> Retire, we have engaged ourselves too far:
> Cæsar himself has work, and our oppression
> Exceeds what we expected.[20]

He and his staff pass, unflurried, across the stage. They have been quickly cured of their confidence. Antony and Scarus pursue them, the youthful elation of Scarus a foil to Antony's self-possession. He is the potent general still, one might believe—set him free from Cleopatra! Drums and alarums subsiding in the distance give us the battle's ending. The emptied stage here is the equivalent of a line of asterisks on a printed page. Then with

Enter Antony again in a march.

comes the brilliant consummation of this last day of good
fortune that he is to see. It ends as it began, with
trumpets sounding; and it has shown us Antony at his
best, generous, gallant, a born leader of men.

Cæsar's sentries on their watch mark the second night's
passing; and our sight of Enobarbus, sick of his ague,
broken in spirit, crawling out into the misty moonlight
to die, gives it a dreary colouring. The dawn breaks dully.

Drums afar off.
> Hark, the drums
> Demurely wake the sleepers. . . .

The armies parade again. First Antony leads his across.
He is smiling grimly, yet there is a desperate edge to his

> I would they'd fight i' the fire, or i' the air;
> We'd fight there too. . . .

Then we see Cæsar, sober caution itself this time. He
passes, heading his men, and the stage stays empty a
moment.

Antony and Scarus appear alone. No tokens of fighting
so far, and Antony is in suspense. With

> Yet they are not joined: where yond pine does stand
> I shall discover all: I'll bring thee word
> Straight, how 'tis like to go.

he vanishes, leaving Scarus to turn suspense to misgiving
with

>   Swallows have built
>   In Cleopatra's sails their nests: the augurers
>   Say they know not, they cannot tell; look grimly,
>   And dare not speak their knowledge. Antony

Is valiant and dejected, and, by starts,
His fretted fortunes give him hope and fear
Of what he has and has not.

Through this comes sounding an

Alarum afar off, as at a sea-fight.

—to our remembrance, a most ominous sound. And
hard upon it, transformed, wrought to a grand climac-
teric of fury, Antony reappears.

All is lost!
This foul Egyptian hath betrayed me:
My fleet hath yielded to the foe; and yonder
They cast their caps up and carouse together
Like friends long lost. Triple-turned whore! 'tis thou
Hast sold me to this novice; and my heart
Makes only wars on thee. Bid them all fly!
For when I am revenged upon my charm,
I have done all. Bid them all fly: begone.[21]

From now till he is carried exhausted and dying to
the Monument Antony's passion dominates the action.
Eros, Mardian, the Guard, Dercetas, Diomedes are
caught distractedly in the wind of it; we see nothing of
Cæsar; panic quickly obliterates Cleopatra. It is a long
passage and highly charged; but Shakespeare can find
all the change and variety he needs in its own turbulent
ebb and flow. Nor, when the medium is rhetoric raised
to such a pitch and given such colouring, could any
competition be admitted; the audience must be caught
and rapt by the mood. The shock of the first outburst
should capture us. Then, the brilliant Scarus, Enobarbus'
successor, Antony's new right hand, having been sent
packing like a lackey (and as ready to go: or do we
wrong him?) we are held by the simple magnificence of

> Oh, sun, thy uprise shall I see no more:
> Fortune and Antony part here; even here
> Do we shake hands. All come to this? The hearts
> That spanieled me at heels, to whom I gave
> Their wishes, do discandy, melt their sweets
> On blossoming Cæsar; and this pine is barked
> That over-topped them all.

His fury soon begins to work again; it is like yeast in him; and when he turns, expectant of Eros coming to his call, to find Cleopatra herself, he chokes for a moment, long enough for her smooth incongruity,

> Why is my lord enraged against his love?

to give a fresh twist to his torture. In this babyish line, and in her flabbergasted, tongue-tied, sudden, very unqueenlike bolting, in his frenzied pursuit of her, Shakespeare again skirts the ridiculous; and closely enough this time to provoke in us a sort of half-hysteria which will attune us to his next shift of key—into the delirium which brings Antony, exhausted, to a pause. We must picture the actor, transfigured to the terms of

> The shirt of Nessus is upon me: teach me,
> Alcides, thou mine ancestor, thy rage:
> Let me lodge Lichas on the horns o' the moon. . . .

and storming from the stage. While we still hear him we see Cleopatra with her scared women and her sapless eunuch scurrying across like rabbits. And as they vanish he follows, vertiginous, insensate! It is a wild, roundabout chase, hazardously raised to poetic power.

If we were not first thrown off our emotional balance we might find the fantasy that follows—for all its beauty—too much an intellectual conceit, and too long-drawn-out.

ANT. Eros, thou yet behold'st me?

EROS.   Ay, noble lord.

ANT. Sometime we see a cloud that's dragonish,
 A vapour sometime like a bear or lion,
 A tower'd citadel, a pendent rock,
 A forked mountain, or blue promontory
 With trees upon't, that nod unto the world
 And mock our eyes with air: thou hast seen these signs;
 They are black vesper's pageants.

EROS.   Ay, my lord.

ANT. That which is now a horse, even with a thought
 The rack dislimns and makes it indistinct,
 As water is in water,

EROS.   It does, my lord.

ANT. My good knave Eros, now thy captain is
 Even such a body. . . .

We should feel with Antony the relief this strange sense
of dissolution brings from the antics of passion, and how,
as he does, one would prolong the respite, playing with
these fancies that the half-freed spirit conceives!

From this he sinks to quiet grief. The sight of the 'saucy
eunuch', on tiptoe with his glib tale, sets fury glowing for
a moment again. Then comes the news, worded as
piteously as ever Cleopatra, safe now in her Monument,
could desire—the news that she is dead. He greets them
as Antony must.[22] The fact that they are false is of a
piece with the other futilities of these three days that have
gone to his undoing. Yet another is to follow when he
stands waiting for the merciful sword-stroke which Eros
turns on himself; yet another when he bungles his own,
and has to lie there, begging the guard to dispatch
him—and, instead, off they go and let him lie![23]

With his carrying to the Monument the long phase of
more particularly 'unlocalized' action, germane to the

three days of fighting, ends. We have been 'ideal' spectators, we know what happened, and why; and just such an impression has been made on us as the reality itself would leave behind. It is a great technical achievement, and one of great artistry too.

Cleopatra Against Cæsar

ANTONY dead, the domination of the play passes at once to Cleopatra. She asserts it in the lament over him; a contrast to his stoic greeting of the news of her death. And from now to the end, the action (but for one short scene) is definitely localized in the Monument. As suited, this, to the intensity and cunning of Cleopatra's battle with Cæsar as was diversity of place to the chances and changes of the other; and by contrast made more telling.

But Antony's death leaves Shakespeare to face one obvious problem: how to prevent Cleopatra's coming as an anticlimax. Plutarch is still lavish of material, but it will need some choosing and moulding.

Cæsar is surprised by the news—here is one risk of slackening tension avoided—and shocked into more feeling than we expect of him. Then at once the last round of the play's contest is opened, and we see what the struggle is to be. A humble anonymous messenger comes from Cleopatra, his message as humble. Cæsar sends him back with fair words; and promptly thereafter:

> Come hither, Proculeius; go and say
> We purpose her no shame: give her what comforts
> The quality of her passion shall require,
> Lest in her greatness by some mortal stroke
> She do defeat us; for her life in Rome
> Would be eternal in our triumph. . . .

It is to be Cæsar's wits against Cleopatra's pride and despair. He fought Antony to the death; it may take more generalship to secure Cleopatra alive. Proculeius, we notice, is sent; the one man about Cæsar, said Antony, that Cleopatra was to trust. Is it in some distrust of him (for his own part) that Cæsar sends Gallus too; and, on yet further thought, Dolabella to watch them both, lest Cleopatra wheedle her way round them? It turns out to be Dolabella that needs watching. But here, unfortunately, the text, as we have it, plays us false. There has been cutting and botching, and the niceties of the business we can now only guess at.[24] The main trend of it is clear, though. In their Roman fashion, Gallus and Proculeius add force to diplomacy and manage to capture Cleopatra in her Monument. Proculeius finds a few moments with this tiger in a trap quite enough for him, and gladly gives place to Dolabella.

The passage that follows is a notable one. He fancies himself, does Dolabella; he is a ladies' man, and quite the jailer, surely, for this most wonderful of wantons.

> Most noble Empress, you have heard of me?

is his ingratiating beginning. From a Roman there is flattery in the very title; it owns her Antony's widow and ignores Octavia. She is far from responsive. She sulks and snarls, gives him half a glance, and forthwith breaks into invidious praise of her dead hero. But she knows she can twist the conceited fellow round her finger. She has only to turn to him with a smile, with an 'I thank you, sir', and a 'Nay, pray you, sir', and he promptly betrays his master to her, blurts out that, for all these comforting messages, Cæsar does mean to lead her chained in his Triumph. At which point Cæsar himself appears.

He comes in full state and circumstance, his staff surrounding him, guards clearing the way. And if Cleopatra thinks to impress him in turn, his opening sally might well damp her somewhat. For he faces this marvel among women as she stands there with her mere maids beside her, and coolly asks which of them is the Queen of Egypt. Which? And once it was

> Remember
> If e'er thou look'st on majesty.

The duel of lies that follows—a pretty piece of fighting!—epitomizes this second and subtler struggle. We have Egyptian against Roman now, neither with much simplicity left to shed; but Cleopatra, passionate and unstable, shows a very child beside Cæsar. She kneels, and he raises her. He repeats his smooth promises, and she smiles her gratitude, alive to the worth of them—had she ever doubted it!—thanks to coxcomb Dolabella. But, surely, for a man so very indifferent to her, he is a little anxious to be gone. Has she any hope of winning him, and does he suspect this? It is second nature in her to be wily with men—and to lie. Seleucus and the false inventory of 'money, plate and jewels' make illuminating matter of dispute. Are not these barbarians to be bribed, and tricked too? Cæsar is neither to be tricked—nor shocked by the attempt made on him. And as for her raging and her nobly pathetic attitudes, he counters them, her lies and her flatteries, too, with the same cold smile. She is beaten. Even Seleucus can withstand her scoldings now; it is Cæsar, contemptuously considerate, who orders the man off. She is helpless in his clutches, but for the one sure escape. And he thinks, does he, to lure her from that with his lies? She fawns on him as he leaves her; let him think he has!

> He words me, girls, he words me, that I should not
> Be noble to myself! . . .

If any doubt were left, any chance of yet another of her accustomed conquests, Dolabella—the paltry proof that she still can conquer—comes back to disperse it.

> DOLABELLA. Madam, as thereto sworn by your command,
>   Which my love makes religion to obey,
>   I tell you this: Cæsar through Syria
>   Intends his journey, and within three days
>   You with your children will he send before:
>   Make your best use of this: I have performed
>   Your pleasure and my promise.
> CLEOPATRA.   Dolabella,
>   I shall remain your debtor.[25]

She again makes his name sound beautiful in his ears (it is a name that can be lingered on), perhaps gives him her hand to kiss (he does not pay Thidias' price for the honour) and he goes. Her way is clear now to death.

But she has still to rise to that final, secure nobility, with which the sight of the dead Antony inspired her.

> and then, what's brave, what's noble,
> Let's do it after the high Roman fashion,
> And make death proud to take us. . . .

She climbs there by no straight path. The longing to die never leaves her. But we all long to die at times; and there is much protesting, a stealthy look or so for chances of escape, some backsliding into the old twisted passions; and she must at last lash herself—with, for company, poor frail Iras—through agony and beyond it before she can repose upon

> My resolution's placed, and I have nothing
> Of woman in me: now from head to foot
> I am marble-constant. . . .

Then, for one more mitigation before the play's last tragic height is reached, Shakespeare gives us the countryman and his figs. By now (here is the art of it) Cleopatra is past bitterness or fear, and can smile and take the simple pleasure in his simplicity that we do. She jokes with him. This must have been, if one comes to think of it, not the least of her charms. When she would royally

> Hop forty paces through the public street . . .

how the people—the common people, so despised by Cæsar and the politicians—how evidently they would adore her! It is very right that one of them should bring her the comfort of death in a basket slung on his arm, and that she should trust him, and joke with him, a great lady at her ease.

From this she turns to a queenliness unapproached before.

> Give me my robe, put on my crown; I have
> Immortal longings in me. . . .

Long ago, we learn, a dead king's servants would be slaughtered around him. This is a still more royal death; for Iras' heart breaks silently at the sight of it, and Charmian only lags behind to set a crooked crown straight once again, and to send triumphant mockery echoing to Cæsar's ears.

He accepts his defeat like a gentleman, let us own. The ceremony of his coming matches the ceremony of her dying; and the end of the play, we should note, is sensibly delayed while they stand gazing—tough soldiers that they are—at a queen so strangely throned:

she looks like sleep,
As she would catch another Antony
In her strong toil of grace.

The Staging

THE action makes no extraordinary calls upon an Elizabethan stage as we now think we know it to have been. Two things are noticeable, however. There are, for five-sixths of the play, few definite indications of the use of the inner stage. This keys with the scant localization of the scenes; the inner and upper stages are always likelier to be 'places' than the main stage will be. But the full stage, *i.e.* the main stage with the inner stage curtains open and the inner stage itself accessible, would probably be used from the general entrance of Charmian, Iras, Mardian, Alexas, the Soothsayer and the rest to Antony's departure for Rome; for all Cleopatra's scenes while she sits waiting news of him—and receiving it; for the long scene of reconciliation between Antony and Cæsar; and for the scene in Pompey's galley.[26] The intermediate scenes will be played on the main stage, with the inner stage curtains closed. When the battles begin it looks as if Cleopatra's scenes again employed the inner stage (as hinterland at least to the outer); she and Antony retiring to it or through it at such points as

Some wine within there, and our viands! ...

Let's to supper, come,
And drown consideration.

—the curtains then closing on them. She may come from the inner stage when she welcomes him from his victory; and

Through Alexandria make a jolly march ...

may imply that they all pass back, as if into the city in triumph. Cæsar's scenes, the marching and counter-marching and the swifter coming and going, take place on the main stage, that is clear.[27]

Now comes disputable matter.

Enter Cleopatra and her Maides aloft, with Charmian and Iras.

They are in the Monument, to which, in a moment, the dying Antony has to be hoisted. There are two slight difficulties. The hoisting of a full-grown man ten or twelve feet in the air asks some strength. However, this could be provided ostensibly by the 'and her Maides', actually by stagehands helping from behind the curtains; and Shakespeare makes dramatic capital out of the apparent difficulty. But the upper stage of the public theatre must have had a balustrade at least three feet high. Swinging a dying man over it and lowering him again asks some care. Granted this done with skill and grace, what of the effect of the rest of the scene, of Antony's death and Cleopatra's lament over him, played behind the balustrade as behind bars? Clearly it would be a poor one. The balustrade must, one presumes, have been removed for the occasion or made to swing open, if the ordinary upper stage was used.[28]

When we next see Cleopatra she is obviously still in the Monument; as obviously she is not still upon such an upper stage as we believe the Globe's to have been. Nor is there any sign that—as with Romeo's farewell to Juliet and her encounter with her mother—the acting of the scene began above and finished below. The stage directions, however, are incomplete, and the text may have been altered. In the previous scene Proculeius and Gallus have been sent to parley with Cleopatra and keep her, if they can, from doing herself a mischief.

By the Folio's stage direction only Proculeius arrives. A simple supposition is that he finds her on the inner stage behind a barred gate and speaks to her through it.[29] This at any rate reproduces Plutarch's 'For Proculeius came to the gates that were very thick and strong, and surely barred; but yet there were some craneries through the which her voyce might be heard. . . . ' When she has protested her submission he evidently makes as if to go, with

> This I'll report, dear lady.
> Have comfort, for I know your plight is pitied
> Of him that caused it.

But now, with no other speech nor stage direction intervening, the Folio has

> PRO. You see how easily she may be surpriz'd;
> Guard her till Cæsar come.

Modern editors (following Theobald in the main) give the speech to Gallus, whom they have brought on with Proculeius, and add:

> *Here Proculeius and two of the Guard ascend the*
> *monument by a ladder placed against a window,*
> *and, having descended, come behind Cleopatra.*
> *Some of the Guard unbar and open the gates.*[30]

A minor objection to this is that Gallus in the Folio is *persona muta*; the full speaking strength of the company is, we may well suppose, already employed, and here is a super. A more serious one must be that so much climbing up and climbing down again would take time. There is no concurrent dialogue, and a long pause at such a moment is dramatically unthinkable.[31]

No great difficulty arises if we see Gallus and the guard left at the door while Proculeius advances to the gate that bars the inner stage. Cleopatra would not see them. Let him give them the order quietly as he returns to the door, and, with no climbing involved, they can be upon the inner stage by the back way in a couple of seconds, seize Cleopatra and unbar the gates; and Gallus may well go off to report to Cæsar; his exit as his entrance, if he stays *persona muta*, being a likely omission from stage directions, which would need to be unwontedly elaborate if all this were to be made clear.[32]

The discussion is fairly barren from a modern producer's point of view; he can provide for all these exigencies without violating the text or distorting the action.

But if for this and all the rest of the action the recognized Elizabethan stage does not content him, then he must devise one which will not violate its fundamental liberties and laws—its liberties, above all. He will probably find in the end that he has devised something not so very different. If he is for painted scenes of *Cleopatra's palace, Cæsar's house, Antony's camp, The plain near Actium* and a variety of 'other parts of the same'— well, the reading of this Preface will only have wasted his time. He must somehow provide a staging free from actuality of place; that is his main problem. He may decorate it; but if the decoration distracts us from the hearing of Shakespeare's lines—and they ask, as we have noted, pretty close attention—it will be a positive nuisance. It is a hard problem to solve; for one thing, because self-effacement is the rarest of artistic virtues. And let the decorator set out, however discreetly, to interpret the play in his own terms, if he find himself—and it is an ever-present danger—competing with the actors, the sole interpreters Shakespeare has licensed, then it is he that is the intruder, and he must

retire. Even if his picturesque effects are but an ano-
dyne to our vigilance—and much modern stage decoration is of this sort—they will do the play negative harm.
We need to have our minds kept clear and alert. Still,
if we cannot take the Elizabethan stage for granted
as the Elizabethans did, producer and decorator must
certainly face the problem of providing something that
we can.

Costume

ONCE we are freed from pictures of Rome and Alexandria, brought (so to speak) archaeologically up to date,
the difficulty of costume is not acute.

> Cut my lace, Charmian.

summarizes it, and, upon a narrow view, may be said
almost to exhaust it. Shakespeare's Cleopatra wore a
stomacher of some sort, that is evident. But it is an error
to suppose that Shakespeare dressed all his plays in the
ordinary costume of his time. It is also an error, for that
matter, to suppose that nowadays we all carry accurate
pictures of the past in our minds. Dress Cleopatra as a
Queen of the Tenth Dynasty instead of as an Alexandrian Greek, and how many of us would be the wiser?
Careful research might find us an Alexandrian fashion
plate of the right period with laces to cut (Sir Arthur
Evans has brought us corsets from Knossos), but our
conscientiously Egyptian Cleopatras have so far been left
laceless and waistless, and the line without meaning.

In all this, as in everything else of the sort, the
Elizabethans thought first and last—whether by choice
or necessity—of dramatic profit. It is not likely that
Shakespeare troubled to give a specifically French touch
to *Love's Labour's Lost* and an Italian to *Much Ado About*

Nothing; nor, had his knowledge run to it, would he probably have seen much gain in dressing Romeo and Juliet by 'the paintings of Giotto and his pupils'.[33] But when some dramatic end was to be served it is clear that he did not lack means of a kind, and he used them. In *Macbeth* the Scots and the English can be told apart, British and Romans in *Cymbeline*; and in this play, quite evidently, Roman and Egyptian stood in picturesque contrast. There would be little archaeology about the business and less consistency. We can guess at the sort of figures they made by turning to extant designs for the Court Masques. The theatres could not run, perhaps, to such splendour as that; but they were prosperous, finery was popular, and they probably did pretty well. Rome meant the romantic past, Egypt the exotic East; and Shakespeare would do what he could to capitalize both. The dialogue of the play is coloured with every sort of allusion to the wonders of that far world, from the description of Cleopatra at Cydnus, to the talk of Syria and the Parthians, from the story of Antony in the Alps, from his call to Alcides his ancestor, to tales of 'pyramises' and crocodiles.

We know better about all these things than did Shakespeare; but it is too late now to put him right. We have to interpret, not to correct him; we are committed even to his errors. Our concern is with the Egypt and Rome of his imagination, not of our own. The difference is manifest less in this detail or the other than in the whole texture of the play. Cut the knot of the 'Cut my lace, Charmian' difficulty, and there is still the larger problem. In the National Gallery hangs Paolo Veronese's 'Alexander and the Wife and Daughter of Darius'. This will be very much how Shakespeare saw his Roman figures habited. Antony would wear Alexander's mixture of doublet, breastplate, sandals and hose. Here too is something very like Octavia's costume; and though Cleopatra might be given some Egyptian stigmata, there would still be laces to cut. It is all grievously incorrect; but we do not like the picture less for that, nor are students set to copy it and told to redraw the costume in the light of the latest information available. Its good painting apart, we even gain by its being a Renaissance view of a Classic subject, for the spirit of the picture is in that. Now, no one will contend that by clothing Antony and Cleopatra and Cæsar and ordering their Court and their armies according to our modern imagination we shall crush the dramatic life out of them, for this is rooted far deeper. But we shall at every moment, both on the main issue and in countless little ways, be falsifying Shakespeare, and doing him far more damage than the simple logic of the case implies. We do him, of all dramatists, great damage. For he has an extraordinary faculty of making the great things vivid to us by means of the little things, by just such strokes, in fact, as that

Cut my lace, Charmian.

This play is exceptionally full of them, very homely things; and it is bare chance that one of the finest, Charmian's

Your crown's awry:
I'll mend it, and then play.

does not get us into more sartorial trouble. He has absorbed Rome and Egypt into his own consciousness; but it is a consciousness opening upon his own world, not the historical Antony's, and naturally not upon our vision of that.

Shakespeare in modern dress is as inappropriate as archaeological Shakespeare, and for the same good reason. And the very argument that great drama is not dependent upon its trimmings should surely help us to

accept the trimmings that we find. Cleopatra in a farthingale! The orthodox playgoer may turn pale at the
thought. But surrender to the idea that this is Shakespeare's Cleopatra we are looking at, not the product of
our schoolbooks (is that more difficult than to look up
from our programme and admit that the well-known
Miss Blank, lately seen as Nora in *A Doll's House*, is the
real thing?), and by the end of the first scene the oddity
will be forgotten; and thenceforward we shall be anach-
ronism-proof. There will be one further gain. An historical play of any sort has a double victory to win; the
play's own and a victory over our preconceptions of its
history. The less familiar its figures the better the chance
of the play with us—as a play.

The Music

TRUMPETS and cornets and drums are needed; and the
flourishes, the sounding of a sennet, the beating of the
drums have each their import. Enobarbus is borne away
dying to the sound of *Drummes afarre offe*. A consort of
woodwind is also used. The 'hoboyes' play under the
stage, and their pungent vibrations should make excellent assault on the nerves.

The music for the revels on Pompey's galley is given
to woodwind (the accompaniment of the song included),
trumpets and drums reinforcing it occasionally. The
clamour is insisted on.

> Make battery to our ears with the loud music. . . .
> These drums! these trumpets, flutes, what!
> Let Neptune hear we bid a loud farewell
> To these great fellows: sound and be hanged, sound out!

It is a soldiers' revel. But it never slips from the distinction of poetry; and the song itself—the boy's voice

singing it—is like light beside the darkness of Menas' whisper to Pompey:

> These three world-sharers, these competitors,
> Are in thy vessel: let me cut the cable;
> And, when we are put off, fall to their throats. . . .

The scene falls midway through the play. It is a rest point in the action. Shakespeare has taken care to give it solidity, variety and colour.

Cleopatra calls once for music, but countermands it with her next breath. She would have needed a consort of viols; and it is possible that strings and woodwind both were more than could be always reasonably demanded at one performance.

The Verse and Its Speaking

ROME and its Empire are ever a clarion call to Shakespeare's imagination; and the strength of his answer to it lies in his power to make the alien characters his own. For he leaves them in no classic immunity, casting his care upon their impressive reputations. They must be sifted through his dramatist's conscience; he brings them to terms on the ground of common humanity. What is Cleopatra's passport to tragic heights?

> No more but e'en a woman, and commanded
> By such poor passion as the maid that milks
> And does the meanest chares. . . .

With this, of course, they risk the loss of their conventionally heroic stature. But it is preserved for them by the magic of poetry.

This is literally a sort of magic, by which the vibrations of emotion that the sound of the poetry sets up seem to enlarge its sense, and break the bounds of the theatre to carry us into the lost world of romantic history. Conceive such a story and such characters so familiarly, and then tie their expression to plain prose—Dido will be in danger of becoming a dowdy indeed, and Cleopatra a gypsy. But Shakespeare has travelled far since Mercutio could thus mock Romeo's poetic prowess, and is now himself by no means 'for the numbers that Petrarch flowed in'. He has come to the writing of a verse which combines actuality and power, and is malleable to every diversity of character and mood. Here and there we may begin to feel a strain. Sometimes emotion will not quite vivify thought, which stays constricted or confused; or a too constant repetition of effect or an oversimplifying of simplicity may show fatigue. But Shakespeare has always had the tact to seize on the subject that will best fit his artist's mood, or to adapt mood and method to subject—which, it is not our business to inquire. And in its qualities and defects alike his present method and ability, resourceful, audacious, spontaneous, ripe if to over-ripeness, fit this subject most consummately well.

Big though the task will be, he feels no need to economize his strength. He begins at what a pitch!

> Nay, but this dotage of our general's
> O'erflows the measure; those his goodly eyes,
> That o'er the files and musters of the war
> Have glow'd like plated Mars, now bend, now turn,
> The office and devotion of their view
> Upon a tawny front: his captain's heart,
> Which in the scuffles of great fights hath burst
> The buckles on his breast, reneges all temper,
> And is become the bellows and the fan
> To cool a gipsy's lust.

Ample and virile in substance, consonant in its music! One tremendous sentence, the ends of the lines not answering to pauses either; these, such as they are, fall midway (a bare four of them in nine lines and more, though), so that fresh impulse may overleap the formal division, and the force be the force of the whole. Note, too, the placing of the dominant 'o'erflows the measure' and its complement 'reneges all temper' with the doubled parenthesis between them, and how the 'now bend, now turn' saves this from slackness; how 'files and musters' and 'office and devotion' strengthen the beat of the verse, with 'plated Mars' coming like the sudden blare of a trumpet, and 'burst the buckles on his breast' to sound the exploding indignation which culminates in the deadly

> And is become the bellows and the fan
> To cool a gipsy's lust.

A fairly opulent dramatic allowance for this Philo, of whom we know nothing, are never to see again. But throughout the play we shall find the least considered characters, and on no special occasion, with as meaty stuff—is there a better term for it?—in their mouths. Mæcenas greets Octavia, upon her disillusioned return, with

> Welcome, dear Madam.
> Each heart in Rome does love and pity you:
> Only the adulterous Antony, most large
> In his abominations, turns you off;
> And gives his potent regiment to a trull,
> That noises it against us.

The anonymous legionary, even, has no less vivid and stirring a moment to his share than

> O noble emperor, do not fight by sea;
> Trust not to rotten planks: do you misdoubt
> This sword and these my wounds? Let the Egyptians

And the Phœnicians go a-ducking: we
Have used to conquer, standing on the earth
And fighting foot to foot.

And from Pompey in his first scene (Shakespeare himself well into his stride by this!) comes the full enrichment of

But all the charms of love,
Salt Cleopatra, soften thy waned lip!
Let witchcraft join with beauty, lust with both!
Tie up the libertine in a field of feasts,
Keep his brain fuming; Epicurean cooks
Sharpen with cloyless sauce his appetite;
That sleep and feeding may prorogue his honour
Even till a Lethe'd dullness.

Too much rich writing of this sort would be like Cleopatra's feasts, and clog the march of the action. But when mere argument is in hand we fall back to nothing less pedestrian than Antony's

Sir,
He fell upon me ere admitted: then
Three kings I had newly feasted, and did want
Of what I was i' the morning: but, next day,
I told him of myself; which was as much
As to have asked him pardon. Let this fellow
Be nothing of our strife: if we contend
Out of our question wipe him.

This, and such a passage as Cæsar's somewhat smug

Let's grant it is not
Amiss to tumble in the bed of Ptolemy;
To give a kingdom for a mirth; to sit
And keep the turn of tippling with a slave;
To reel the streets at noon, and stand the buffet
With knaves that smell of sweat; say this becomes him—

As his composure must be rare indeed
Whom these things cannot blemish—yet must Antony
No way excuse his foils, when we do bear
So great weight in his lightness.

or as Pompey's

> To you all three,
> The senators alone of this great world,
> Chief factors for the gods,—I do not know
> Wherefore my father should revengers want,
> Having a son and friends, since Julius Cæsar,
> Who at Philippi the good Brutus ghosted,
> There saw you labouring for him.

may be taken as the norm of the play's poetic method,
upon which its potencies are built up. And it is upon
this norm, of course, that the actors must model their
own style.

The elemental oratory of this verse needs for its
speaking a sense of rhythm that asks no help of strict
rule. Shakespeare is so secure by now in the spirit of its
laws that the letter may go. He does not commonly stray
far. A cæsura may fall oddly or there may be none
distinguishable, a syllable or so may splash over at the
end. Dramatic emphasis is the thing, first and last; to
get that right he will sacrifice strict metre—yet never
music—grammar now and then, and at a pinch, if need
be, exact sense too.

These freedoms gain in effect as the play's temper
heightens. Cæsar's calculated indignation is sounded in
the two swelling catalogues:

> I'the common show place where they exercise.
> His sons he there proclaimed the kings of kings:
> Great Media, Parthia and Armenia
> He gave to Alexander; to Ptolemy he assign'd

Syria, Cilicia and Phœnicia. . . .
                    He hath assembled
Bocchus, the king of Libya; Archelaus
Of Cappadocia. . . .

The latter passage has been quoted already; the scansion is highly individual.

But no Cleopatra, with an ear, can miss the shrill arrogance of

> Sink Rome, and their tongues rot
> That speak against us! A charge we bear i' the war,
> And, as the president of my kingdom, will
> Appear there for a man. Speak not against it;
> I will not stay behind.

The upward run of semiquavers in 'A charge we bear i' the war' is as plain as any musical stave could make it; and the pauses seem to mark so many snaps of the jaw. The lines are not, of course, here or elsewhere to be reckoned by syllables, but by beat.

Listen, on the other hand, to the weary descent to depression's depths in Antony's

> Fall not a tear, I say; one of them rates
> All that is won and lost: give me a kiss;
> Even this repays me. We sent our schoolmaster;
> Is 'a come back? Love, I am full of lead.

—given us by a regular caesura, followed by an irregular one, followed by a mid-line full stop; the line then finished with an effort by the banal 'We sent our schoolmaster' (who could get anything but exhaustion out of that 'schoolmaster'?); the next line with its dead monosyllables dragging after, the pause in the middle made the longer because of them. Then comes a sudden rally in the rhymed couplet:

> Some wine, within there, and our viands! Fortune knows
> We scorn her most when most she offers blows.

—its irregular first line just saving it from sounding mechanical.

The violence of Antony's anger when he finds Thidias kissing Cleopatra's hand has its own notation and tune.

> Approach there! Ah, you kite! Now, gods and devils!
> Authority melts from me. Of late, when I cried 'Ho!',
> Like boys unto a muss, kings would start forth
> And cry 'Your will?' Have you no ears?
> I am Antony yet. Take hence this jack and whip him.

Long lines, giving a sense of great strength. Exclamatory phrases, prefacing and setting off the powerful centre-phrase, with its ringing 'kings' for a top note. The caesura-pause of two beats that the short line allows is followed by the repeated crack of two more short phrases, the first with its upward lift, the second with its nasal snarl and the sharp click of its ending; the last line lengthens out, and the business finishes with the bitten *staccato* of

> Take hence this jack and whip him.

Note the deadly flick of the last two words!

The sense apart, what an almost wilful pathos we feel in the smoothly sustained, one- and two-syllable worded, predominantly thin-vowelled speech of Antony's to the weeping servants!

> Tend me to-night;
> May be it is the period of your duty:
> Haply you shall not see me more; or if,
> A mangled shadow: perchance to-morrow
> You'll serve another master. I look on you
> As one that takes his leave. Mine honest friends,

> I turn you not away; but, like a master
> Married to your good service, stay till death.
> Tend me to-night two hours. I ask no more;
> And the gods yield you for 't.

Note in particular the importance given to 'A mangled shadow' by the sustaining tripled consonant, and the two-beat pause that follows ('to-morrow', with its weak ending, ranking for a dissyllable), and how the repeated, 'Tend me to-night' rounds in the speech a trifle artificially.

Throughout these scenes, throughout the play indeed, one can so analyze the verse, find its rhythm and music, often transcending rule, but always close fitted to mood and meaning. The best moments need no analysis, and seem to defy it. One must not appear to be praising.

> I am dying, Egypt, dying; only
> I here importune death awhile, until
> Of many thousand kisses the poor last
> I lay upon thy lips.
>   I dare not, dear—,
> Dear, my lord, pardon,—I dare not,
> Lest I be taken:

merely for the way in which a short first line allows for the two silent breaths that will show Antony's flagging strength, nor for the infallible accenting of Cleopatra's fear, first upon the 'dare', and then, with repetition, upon the 'not'. But actors have to concern themselves with such impertinences.

The passionate hysteria of her

> Where art thou, death?
> Come hither, come! come, come, and take a queen
> Worth many babes and beggars!
> PROCULEIUS. O, temperance, lady!

CLEOPATRA. Sir, I will eat no meat, I'll not drink, sir—
   If idle talk will once be necessary—
   I'll not sleep neither: this mortal house I'll ruin. . . .

asks neither comment nor analysis. Why waste time trying to scan the last line? It is right, and not the extremest perversity could speak it wrongly, one would suppose. Nor will much more be gained by trying to extract meaning from the last line but one. If it has any in particular (which seems doubtful) no audience could be made to grasp it. But as a setting of hysterical gibbering to verbal music, it is perfect.

But one technical excellence among many it is hard to pass by. As Shakespeare nears the last great moment, that of Cleopatra's death, he wants to give his verse solid strength and dignity; and the pulse of it now throbs with a steady intensity, goes processionally forward, as it were.

Give me my robe, put on my crown; I have
Immortal longings in me: now no more
The juice of Egypt's grape shall moist this lip.
Yare, yare, good Iras: quick! Methinks I hear
Antony call; I see him rouse himself
To praise my noble act; I hear him mock
The luck of Cæsar, which the gods give men
To excuse their after wrath. . . .

Regular metre, saved from formality by the subtle variety of the mid-line stopping; the whole welded into unity by the constant carrying-on of the sentences from line to line. But, lest the effect grow all too set, Charmian is let interpose, a little later, not a single line but one and a half. Then, lest life die out of it, we have—after the added emphasis of an irregular line, in which Cleopatra lays hands on the asp with a heavily accentuated 'Come . . .'—the words clipped, the pace quickened. Twice more Charmian interrupts, but now with phrases that sustain rather than break the rhythm.

> CLEOPATRA. Come, thou mortal wretch,
>   With thy sharp teeth this knot intrinsicate
>   Of life at once untie; poor venomous fool,
>   Be angry, and despatch. O, could'st thou speak,
>   That I might hear thee call great Cæsar ass
>   Unpolicied!
> CHARMIAN.   O eastern star!
> CLEOPATRA.   Peace, peace!
>   Dost thou not see my baby at my breast,
>   That sucks the nurse asleep?
> CHARMIAN.   O break! O break!
> CLEOPATRA. As sweet as balm, as soft as air, as gentle!
>   O, Antony!—Nay, I will take thee too:
>   What should I stay—?

Not one beat has been missed till her dying breaks the last line; yet we have been no more conscious of the form than when the verse was at its loosest, only of the added power.

Shakespeare no longer divides his characters into speakers of verse and speakers of prose, nor makes this distinction regularly between scenes. The freedom and variety of his verse writing allow him to pass almost imperceptibly from poetry to prose and back again. Thus he ranges an unbroken scale, from a pedestrian exactitude in stating plain fact at one end of it to the conventional flourish of the rhymed couplet at the other. But he can still make the sharp contrast of a change effective between scene and scene; or in the midst of a scene he can bring passion or pretentiousness down to earth—and prose, or as suddenly restore force and dignity with rhythm and tone. And he can go to work more subtly than that. As in stagecraft, so in his play's actual writing, exploiting freedom to the full, he has forged a weapon of extraordinary suppleness and resource.

For instance, in the ostensibly prose scene that follows the play's more formal opening, we have the Soothsayer countering Charmian's impudent chatter with single lines of verse. Their recurrence lends him peculiarity and a slight portentousness; but the surrounding prose is so subtly adjusted that the device itself passes unnoticed.[34] Later, upon Cleopatra's entrance, the scene is suddenly braced to forcefulness by half a dozen consecutive lines of (not too regular, lest the effect be too noticeable) verse. Later still, with a strong dose of prose, Enobarbus turns Antony's philosophic realism very much the seamy side out.

Enobarbus (he in particular) speaks now verse, now prose, either as the scene requires it of him for harmony or contrast, or as his humours dictate; his character being just such a compound of contrasts. Antony only occasionally relapses to prose, and his verse is regular on the whole. Cleopatra hardly touches prose at all; her verse is apt to be a little freer. Cæsar speaks only verse; it is fairly formal, and expressive of his calculated dignity.

But the supreme virtue of the writing lies in its peculiar combination of delicacy and strength, of richness with simplicity. For simple strength take the quick passage in which Menas tempts Pompey to put to sea and then cut the throats of his guests.

MENAS. Wilt thou be lord of all the world?
POMPEY.   What say'st thou?
MENAS. Wilt thou be lord of the whole world? That's twice.
POMPEY. How should that be?
MENAS.   But entertain it,
  And though thou think me poor, I am the man
  Will give thee all the world.

For simplicity, Cleopatra's

O well-divided disposition! Note him,
Note him, good Charmian, 'tis the man; but note him.
He was not sad, for he would shine on those
That make their looks by his; he was not merry;
Which seemed to tell them his remembrance lay
In Egypt with his joy; but between both:
O heavenly mingle!

For delicacy, her

But bid farewell and go: when you sued staying,
Then was the time for words: no going then;
Eternity was in our lips and eyes,
Bliss in our brows' bent; none our parts so poor,
But was a race of heaven. . . .

or Antony's

Come, let's all take hands;
Till that the conquering wine hath steeped our sense
In soft and delicate Lethe.

or his picture of Octavia:

Her tongue will not obey her heart, nor can
Her heart inform her tongue—the swan's down-feather,
That stands upon the swell at the full of tide,
And neither way inclines.

For strength, his malediction of Cleopatra:

You were half-blasted ere I knew you; ha!
Have I my pillow left unpressed in Rome,
Forborne the getting of a lawful race,
And by a gem of women, to be abused
By one that looks on feeders?

or his dismissal of the half-flayed Thidias.

Get thee back to Cæsar;
Tell him thy entertainment: look thou say

> He makes me angry with him; for he seems
> Proud and disdainful, harping on what I am,
> Not what he knew I was. He makes me angry;
> And at this time most easy 'tis to do't,
> When my good stars, that were my former guides,
> Have empty left their orbs, and shot their fires
> Into the abysm of hell.

We constantly have that favourite device, the enrichment of a simple effect by an echoing phrase; as when Cleopatra turns to Antony in pathetic dignity with

> Sir, you and I must part, but that's not it:
> Sir, you and I have loved, but there's not it. . . .

—as in the Soothsayer's response to Antony's command to him to speak no more:

> To none but thee; no more, but when to thee.

The thought also is echoed in Cleopatra's

> That time—O, times!—
> I laughed him out of patience; and that night
> I laughed him into patience: and next morn
> Ere the ninth hour, I drunk him to his bed. . . .

and in Enobarbus' remorseful

> This blows my heart:
> If swift thought break it not, a swifter mean
> Shall outstrike thought: but thought will do't, I feel.

Such devices easily degenerate into trick; as this comes near to doing with Cleopatra's

> These hands do lack nobility, that they strike
> A meaner than myself; since I myself
> Have given myself the cause.

—even as the power of concentration which can pack three clear thoughts into those seven words of hers:

> Therefore be deaf to my unpitied folly. . . .

has overreached itself a moment earlier in

> O, my oblivion is a very Antony,
> And I am all forgotten.

The most delicate and precise accenting of the 'oblivion' and the 'all' may fail to make the meaning of this last clear upon the instant.

But we have concentration, clarity, strength, simplicity all combined in the swift exchange between Alexas and Cleopatra when he brings her the first news of the absent Antony with

> His speech sticks in my heart.
> Mine ear must pluck it thence.

she answers; and in her dark misgiving as the unlucky second messenger faces her:

> But, sirrah, mark, we use
> To say the dead are well: bring it to that,
> The gold I give thee I will melt and pour
> Down thy ill-uttering throat.

and in the primitive

> Call the slave again:
> Though I am mad, I will not bite him: call!

Such things seem easy only when they are done—and well done.

Again, there is artistry of the subtlest in the freedom and apparent ease of this (the same wretched messenger is now atoning for his fault by disparaging Octavia, Charmian abetting him):

MESSENGER. She creeps:
  Her motion and her station are as one;
  She shows a body rather than a life,
  A statue than a breather.
CLEOPATRA. Is this certain?
MESSENGER. Or I have no observance.
CHARMIAN. Three in Egypt
  Cannot make better note.
CLEOPATRA. He's very knowing;
  I do perceive 't: there's nothing in her yet;
  The fellow has good judgment.
CHARMIAN. Excellent.
CLEOPATRA. Guess at her years, I prithee.
MESSENGER. Madam,
  She was a widow.—
CLEOPATRA. Widow! Charmian, hark!

—in the way the continuing swing of the verse keeps the
dialogue swift while the dividing of the lines gives spontaneity.

Note how actual incoherence—kept within bounds by
the strict rhythm of the verse—leads up to, and trebles
the nobility of a culminating phrase. (She and her
women surround the dead Antony.)

          How do you, women?
  What, what, good cheer? Why, how now, Charmian!
  My noble girls! Ah women, women, look!
  Our lamp is spent, it's out. Good sirs, take heart:
  We'll bury him; and then, what's brave, what's noble,
  Let's do it after the high Roman fashion,
  And make death proud to take us. . . .

The compelled swiftness of the beginning, the change
without check when she turns to the soldiers, the accord-
ant discipline of the line which follows, so that the last

two lines can come out clarion-clear; here, again, is dramatic music exactly scored. In like fashion Antony's mixed metaphors (when he has been told she is dead), which include something very like a pun, lead up to and enhance a luminous close.

> I will o'ertake thee, Cleopatra, and
> Weep for my pardon. So it must be, for now
> All length is torture: since the torch is out,
> Lie down and stray no farther: now all labour
> Mars what it does: yea, very force entangles
> Itself with strength: seal then, and all is done.
> Eros!—I come, my queen: Eros!—Stay for me:
> Where souls do couch on flowers, we'll hand in hand,
> And with our sprightly port make the ghosts gaze:
> Dido and her Æneas shall want troops,
> And all the haunt be ours.

While, for a glorious and famous passage that is music itself—but what more?—take:

> O see, my women,
> The crown o' the earth doth melt. My lord!
> O, withered is the garland of the war,
> The soldier's pole is fall'n: young boys and girls
> Are level now with men; the odds is gone,
> And there is nothing left remarkable
> Beneath the visiting moon.

This, in analysis, is little better than ecstatic nonsense; and it is meant to sound so. It has just enough meaning in it for us to feel as we hear it that it may have a little more. Art must by so much at least improve on nature; in nature it would have less or none. But it gives us to perfection the reeling agony of Cleopatra's mind; therefore, in its dramatic setting, it ranks as supreme poetry.

Utterly sure of himself, Shakespeare has, in fine, reached in the writing as in the shaping of this play limits of freedom and daring that he will not, but for the worse, overpass.

The Characters

ANTONY

IN the two early episodes of his breaking from Egypt and of his welcome to Rome Antony is painted for us in breadth and detail; they give us the man complete, and thereafter the drama of his actions needs no alloy of analysis or explanation.

Shakespeare's first strokes seldom fail to be significant. The four words to the messenger, who crosses Antony's uncharted path as he and Cleopatra saunter by, with

> News, my good lord, from Rome.
> Grates me! The sum?

(the harsh, impatient, yet slightly conscience-stricken sound of it!); the next three to Cleopatra:

> How, my love?

(the softened vowels!), then the full diapason of the heroic, yet fustian-flavoured

> Let Rome in Tiber melt, and the wide arch
> Of the ranged empire fall! . . .

—here, in a few phrases, we have the gallant grown old and the confident conqueror in decline. He passes on; the keynote has been struck. But Philo's sad, scrupulous

> Sir, sometimes when he is not Antony,
> He comes too short of that great property
> Which still should go with Antony.

promises, and Cleopatra's descent upon her giggling maids preludes another tune in him with

CLEOPATRA. Saw you my lord?
ENOBARBUS.   No, lady.
CLEOPATRA.   Was he not here?
CHARMIAN. No, madam.
CLEOPATRA. He was disposed to mirth; but on the sudden
A Roman thought hath struck him. . . .

She sees him coming and will have him see her go, her offended nose in the air. But if he does he ignores her.[35]

The so-lately snubbed messenger is with him, talking, and encouraged to, as man to man. (These messengers, by the bye, are not errand boys, but men of responsibility.) This is the Antony—or little less than he—that could cooly outface and out-scheme the mob of Cæsar's murderers, outgeneral the ideologue Brutus and Cassius the fanatic; it is Antony the realist, and never a starker one than when he needs to see himself coldly and clearly as he is. And he is enough a master of men to dare to let them see him so!

Who tells me true, though in his tale lie death,
I hear him as he flattered.

This encounter with the messengers sets him very relentlessly before us. Shakespeare has never had more illusions about Antony than he about himself. In *Julius Cæsar* how swiftly the heroics of the Capitol and the flattering eloquence of the Forum were followed by the calm proposal to Lepidus and Octavius to cheat the citizens, whose hearts he had just won, of part of their legacies; and, Lepidus being sent on this errand, to jockey *him* next out of his share of the spoils. But, whatever he was at, there was a sportsmanlike gaiety about him then. He has grown colder with the years,

cynically philosophical. It is a quality of greatness in a
man, no doubt, that seeks the truth and sees it even in
himself, boldly lets others see it. But such truth, seen
and shown with such indifference! Colder; and callous,
one adds.

The second messenger's appearance is heralded by
ominous hesitations. (The play abounds in these deli-
cacies of craftsmanship.) And, when he does appear,
Antony, by that unusual

> What are you?

reads trouble in the sight of him. The answer comes
straight:

> Fulvia thy wife is dead.

The response, the curt question,

> Where died she?

makes no sentimental pretences; and, the messenger
dismissed, he is as honest with himself.

> There's a great spirit gone! Thus did I desire it.
> What our contempts doth often hurl from us,
> We wish it ours again: the present pleasure
> By revolution lowering, does become
> The opposite of itself.—She's good, being gone....

And Enobarbus, summoned to make ready for departure, is in talk with him a minute or more before,
casually abrupt, he says

> Fulvia is dead.
> Sir?
> Fulvia is dead.
> Fulvia!
> Dead.

We recall Brutus and Cassius and Portia's death.[36] This also, then, would seem to be in 'the high Roman fashion'. But how truly English, too, the avoidance of the subject, the curt exchange to hide emotion—which, it may be, is not there to hide!

Enobarbus' frank brutalities lend by contrast dignity to his chief, as, lost now in 'Roman thoughts', he passes on to take his leave of Cleopatra. He knows her

> cunning past man's thought . . .

He is free of her forever if he would be; and it is hardly, one would say, a very fatal passion that shows in his farewell. He looks for tantrums.

> I am sorry to give breathing to my purpose. . . .

An uncomfortably polite opening; it is an awkward business.

She plays her every pretty trick on him; but she can tell that the Roman thought has, for the moment, conquered.[37] His protests come easily; she makes short work of them. She stirs him to candour by twitting him with 'Liar'; but she unmasks more reality than she bargained for.

> Hear me, queen.
> The strong necessity of time commands
> Our services awhile. . . .

—and when Antony bites thus on his words, it is as well to be silent and listen. We are at the pivot of the scene, its revealing moment. He unfolds for her, with all the force of his mind, his tangled task ahead. She listens indifferently: what are politics and Sextus Pompeius to her? Then he adds—as if it were an item forgotten in the sum—

> My more particular,
> And that which most with you should safe my going,
> Is Fulvia's death.

Spoiled wanton of a woman she may be, but she has a
sensitiveness he lacks and a humanity he has lost. On
the instant there possesses her such a sense of the pitiful
transient littleness of life:

> Though age from folly could not give me freedom
> It does from childishness. Can Fulvia 'die'?

—of her own life too, and of their love:

> Now I see, I see,
> In Fulvia's death, how mine received shall be.

Yet the next instant she is trifling it away and at her
tricks again.

The duel goes on, he obstinately asserting that it is all
to her queenly advantage he should go, she pricking and
stinging him with her woman's grievances. She cannot
change his purpose, but she knows how to conquer in
retreat.

> But, sir, forgive me,
> Since my becomings kill me when they do not
> Eye well to you! Your honour calls you hence:
> Therefore be deaf to my unpitied folly,
> And all the gods go with you. Upon your sword
> Sit laurel victory! and smooth success
> Be strewed before your feet!

That, she sees to it, shall be his remembrance of her.

He is found next in Rome, confronting Cæsar and
out-topping him; and by how much more the lesser men
around, Lepidus, Agrippa, Mæcenas and the rest. In this
scene and those deriving from it we have Antony at his

ablest, the seasoned statesman. That prefatory hint at his soldiership, peaceably though he now comes,

>   'Tis spoken well,
>   Were we before our armies and to fight,
>   I should do thus.

the quick opening of the argument, when courtesies with Cæsar have been exchanged,

>   I learn, you take things ill that are not so,
>   Or, being, concern you not.

give him vantage of position. He has, it would appear, a poor enough case to plead. He makes neither useless defence nor impulsive apology, but with clever dialectic shapes the issue, as far as may be, to his liking. Cæsar is pettish, but Antony—diplomatist that he is—remains proof against pin-pricks. He even jokes about the dead Fulvia and her 'garboils'.

>   As for my wife,
>   I would you had her spirit in such another.
>   The third o' the world is yours, which with a snaffle
>   You may pace easy, but not such a wife.

He makes shrugging confession of his own failings; and in all so takes the wind out of Cæsar's sails that that self-conscious respectability is stung at last into taxing this elderly scapegrace point blank with perjury—very much to Lepidus' alarm. Antony still stays unruffled. But, with his adversary trapped into such rashness, we can feel his wrist harden and see the steely eye above the easy smile.

>   No,
>   Lepidus, let him speak:
>   The honour is sacred which he talks on now,

> Supposing that I lacked it. But, on, Cæsar;
> The article of my oath.

Cæsar does not shirk; but he speaks now by the card.
Antony (in his own phrase) paces them all with a snaffle.
Let them take no liberties, though. He may jest about
Egypt; they had better not.

Then Mæcenas and Agrippa take up their allotted part
in the peacemaking. The marriage with Octavia is
broached.

> great Mark Antony
> Is now a widower.

The outmatched Cæsar cannot resist a malicious gibe.

> Say not so, Agrippa:
> If Cleopatra heard you, your reproof
> Were well deserved of rashness.

He earns the snub direct.

> I am not married, Cæsar: let me hear
> Agrippa further speak.

But business is business, and a peace is patched up
between the two, 'according to plan'.

From now to the consummating of the treaty with
Pompey, and thereafter to the brotherly parting with
Cæsar, Antony stands in the sun. These men know his
worth to them and he knows it. Secure in reputation,
he can be generous to Pompey, who girds at him too;
he is even civil to Lepidus. And he brings to Octavia
such a boyish penitence—

> My Octavia,
> Read not my blemishes in the world's report:
> I have not kept my square; but that to come
> Shall all be done by the rule.

—that how should we not, with the good Mæcenas, trust to her beauty, wisdom and modesty to settle his chastened heart? But Enobarbus has warned us betimes; and we see him, on the instant, turn from her to the Soothsayer, that sinister shadow of his bewitchment; and the very next we hear is

> I will to Egypt:
> And though I make this marriage for my peace,
> I' the East my pleasure lies.

He is lost. And the significant thing is that he sinks without an effort from sanity to folly. He has won back his lost ground. We have seen him, with easy authority, outmatching Cæsar, and Cæsar, for all his jealousy, shrewdly content to be outmatched. Yet here he is flinging everything away. This is not the Antony of Philippi, of the Capitol and the Forum. His spirit all afraid to govern him near Cæsar! Is it, indeed!? Cæsar has all the luck at dicing and cockfighting. No doubt! But the naked truth is that the sensual man in him must find excuse for the

> I will to Egypt. . . .
> I' the East my pleasure lies.

and any is better than none.

This is the nemesis of the sensual man. Till now Antony's appetites have not fatally played him false. Such gifts and vitality as his can for long enough make the best of both worlds, the sensual and the world of judgment too; for life is bred in passion, and has continuing need of it. But the time comes when Nature finds no more profit in a man, and her saving graces fail him. Antony has never learned to bargain with life; his abundant strength could take politics and love-affairs, interest and inclination in its stride. And now that judgment does pull one way and appetite another there is neither struggle nor dispute, no overt choice made, even. Appetite wins, while judgment winks and ignores defeat. He knows what going back to Cleopatra means.

> These strong Egyptian fetters I must break,
> Or lose myself in dotage.

Yet in the very knitting-up of the new ties that are to save him from her he can say, 'I'll go', nor seem to count the cost. He speaks his own doom in a careless phrase—and forgets it. He will have his chance to make a brave show still and a nobler end; but shameful, secret moments such as this are the true counterpart to that earlier conscienceless success. No agony, nor darkening of the spirit before defeat, nor a Promethean defiance of the partial gods. This hero's fate is sealed quite casually, in a talk with a soothsayer about dice and fighting cocks.

Shakespeare adds yet one more touch to his disintegrating. Antony, we shall remember, came with Ventidius to the conference, saying

> If we compose well here, to Parthia.

—to avenge his Egypt-bred defeats there. But now it is

> O, come, Ventidius,
> *You* must to Parthia.

while he will wait the chance to step back to his sty.

This phase of the study of him, in sober businesslike relation to Cæsar and his fellow-Romans, gives great ballast to the play. Cleopatra's hectic scenes stand in current contrast to it, and it is steadying preparation for the violence of the end. It is prose in its temper, but the pitch and swing of the actual verse lend it a more heroic life. There come no exciting clashes; but these close-woven contrasts of character that are its substance are the very stuff of drama.

Shakespeare is never the vindictive moralist, scourging a man with his sins, blind to all else about him. Antony's ending, when we reach it, is of a piece with his life. It is the garment of his good fortune turned inside out; and if some virtues have more lustre, some vices are more tolerable in failure than success. Once again, here is no spiritual tragedy of ideals betrayed. The man has had what he wanted from the world; with luck, daring and judgment to bring it him. A debauched judgment, no luck left to draw upon, mere daring become folly, and he loses it; that is the whole story. But he loses like a man, and there is some spiritual tragedy in it too; for if no ideals betray him, yet at every turn he is conscious that he betrays himself. He knows—who better?—that he should not fight Cæsar by sea. He has no reasons to give but

> For that he dares us to't.

All his answer to argument, as he stands supine under Cleopatra's eye, is a weakly obstinate

> By sea, by sea!

though he adds, for excuse, a futile

> But if we fail,
> We then can do't at land.

His mind seems a blank. He has no plan of battle; and with one defeat his nerve and self-respect are gone.

This is his lowest fall, and there in helpless ignominy we might have to leave him

> unqualitied with very shame . . .

to humble himself before his conqueror, to

> dodge
> And palter in the shifts of lowness . . .

—but for Cæsar! Thanks to his enemy, the old courage and a new nobility are made to stir in him. There is a cold unloveliness about Cæsar. With Antony at his mercy—well, he might accord it or refuse it; but surely he need not so promptly send an envoy to win Cleopatra from him who has lost everything for her sake, to tempt her at any price to drive from Egypt

> her all-disgraced friend,
> Or take his life there . . .

Conquerors, it would seem, cannot even learn the common sense of magnanimity. The clever trick comes near, though, to costing Cæsar all he has won and more.

Antony has been no great precisian in such matters himself; but he is thinking now, we may suppose, less of his own shortcomings than of old days of comradeship with Cæsar when the diffident schoolmaster-ambassador returns.

> Is *that* his answer?
> Ay, my lord.
> The queen shall then have courtesy, so she
> Will yield us up.
> He says so.
> Let her know't.

He recovers some at least of his stature as hero with that.

But if this is not spiritual tragedy, still less is it a moral tale, with the scales of vice and virtue neatly tipped for our edifying; Shakespeare has left all that behind with artifice of plot and characters cut to suit it. The light is shining for us here upon things as they were and men as they are. So the heroic gesture can be followed by the folly of the challenge to Cæsar and the savagery of the whipping of Thidias; by the bitter purging of the illusion that was Cleopatra, and at her beck, the prompt re-embracing of it with a narcotic

> I am satisfied.

Yet if Cleopatra is all that in his fury he says she is, and even readier, it may be, to betray him than he thinks, she is not cold-hearted toward him, strange though that may seem.[38] And while (by every rule of ready-made morality) his open-eyed return to bondage and debauch should bring him swiftly to defeat,—and fact-facing Enobarbus makes sure it will—on the contrary, it preludes temporary victory, and it is the over-confident Cæsar that must learn a lesson.

But Cæsar is quick to learn, and Enobarbus will prove right in the end (though remorse and malaria end him before he finds it out), and Shakespeare forthwith shows us very plainly the flaws in the prospect. There is the omen of the strange music that the soldiers hear, the sign that

> the god Hercules, whom Antony loved,
> Now leaves him.[39]

and the strange mood in Antony himself that sets him, on the eve of battle, to making his followers weep his likely death.

> The gods make this a happy day to Antony!

is the old legionary's greeting to him as he marches out in the morning; and the response is generous:

> Would thou and those thy scars had once prevailed
> To make me fight at land!

The gods do grant him one more happy day, and we see him at his best in it. Shakespeare shows it as the briefest of the three; a ray shooting through sunset clouds.

He begins it with what may be called the single touch of romantic sentiment in the play. Antony and Cleopatra come out in the early dawn—come from a night of revel, moreover!—like a young bride and bridegroom, laughing together at her pretty fumblings as she helps him put his armour on. A spoiled child's useless fingers; Octavia would have made a neater job of it, one fears! He flatters and pets her:

> Well, well:
> We shall thrive now!

Her glee when she has slipped a strap into place!

> Is not this buckled well?
>   Rarely, rarely! . . .
> Thou fumblest, Eros, and my queen's a squire
> More tight at this than thou.

Seen among his soldiers he is still the Antony of her worship:

> The demi-Atlas of this earth, the arm
> And burgonet of men.

But there are qualities in him that a little pass her understanding, perhaps. For, even as he sets forth, he learns that Enobarbus has deserted; and, very quietly, with no touch of anger, and but one most human shade of bitterness, comes

>   What say'st thou?
> SOLDIER.   Sir,
>   He is with Cæsar.

EROS.　　　　　　　Sir, his chests and treasure
　He has not with him.
ANTONY.　　　　　Is he gone?
SOLDIER.　　　　　　　　Most certain.
ANTONY. Go, Eros, send his treasure after; do it;
　Detain no jot, I charge thee: write to him—
　I will subscribe—gentle adieus and greetings;
　Say that I wish he never find more cause
　To change a master. O, my fortunes have
　Corrupted honest men! Despatch. Enobarbus!

He goes to fight, not confident of the issue (not stained
with such overconfidence as Cæsar's, certainly), nor
braggart of his cause. And when he beats his enemy and
returns in triumph, his first thought is to thank his
soldiers and to praise before them all the young and
wounded Scarus, the hero of the day, who, for his
reward, shall kiss Cleopatra's hand. Does she remember
Thidias at this juncture, and *his* wounds?

　Not much is made of the third day's fighting; nor does
Shakespeare trouble with the question which Plutarch
leaves unanswered, whether Cleopatra did 'pack cards'
with Cæsar or no. It is enough that fortune crashes upon
Antony in final ruin. There is little noble about him now,
in his beastlike rage and thirst for her blood; much
though that is pitiful in the wreck of such a man.

　　　The soul and body rive not more in parting
　　　Than greatness going off.

For, if but in his folly, he has been great. He has held
nothing back, has flung away for her sake honour and
power, never weighing their worth against her worthless-
ness; there is a sort of selfless greatness in that. The lust
to kill her before he kills himself is the due backwash of
such spendthrift love. He sees her and cannot; folly is

folly and weakness is weakness still, he can only damn
her to a shamefuller end. Fury racks him again; and
then the merciful riving of spirit from body begins.
Shakespeare turns, as we have seen, to pure poetry to
express it:

> ANTONY. Eros, thou yet beholdest me?
> EROS.   Ay, noble lord.
> ANTONY. Sometimes we see a cloud that's dragonish. . . .

He is coming to the end of his strength—even his!—and
the body's passions begin to seem unreal, and he to be
slipping free of them. Yet another wrench or so of anger,
suffering and shame; and the news comes that, in despite
of him, she it is that has slipped free.

It is a lie; and he will be a laughingstock in death.
What more fitly tragic end for the brilliant general and
statesman, the great realist and paragon of worldly wisdom, than to be tricked into emulating the heroism of
a Cleopatra, who is, we know, even now safe in her
Monument; than to be outdone in quiet courage by his
servant; than to bungle his own death-stroke and have
to lie begging, in vain, to be put out of his misery? And,
as he lies there, he learns the ridiculous truth.

Shakespeare spares him no ignominy; yet out of it
rises, not, to be sure, an Antony turned angel, but a man
set free of debt to fate, still abiding in his faith, justified
of it, then, at the last. When the news of Cleopatra's
death comes, he reproaches her no more, says not a
word of any loss but this, has no thought but to follow
her. What purpose is left him?

> Unarm, Eros; the long day's task is done,
> And we must sleep.

He is nothing without her; the world is empty and time
has no meaning.

> Since Cleopatra died,
> I have lived in such dishonour, that the gods
> Detest my baseness. . . .

Since she died, the single minute's passing has been to him as years. And when, dying, he learns that she lives he makes no comment upon that; what do Fate's pettinesses matter now? He asks only to be carried to her that he may die in her arms. Even of this he comes near to being cheated. She will not risk her safety for his sake. But she has them draw him up to her; and his thoughts are for her safety and peace of mind.

> The miserable change now at my end
> Lament nor sorrow at; but please your thoughts
> In feeding them with those my former fortunes,
> Wherein I lived the greatest prince o' the world,
> The noblest; and do now not basely die,
> Not cowardly put off my helmet to
> My countryman—a Roman by a Roman
> Valiantly vanquished. Now my spirit is going;
> I can no more.

He has loved her, the worst and the best of her; and given her the best and the worst of him. He won much from the world, so he had much to lose. Losers ought not to whine. Antony stays a soldier and a sportsman—and a gentleman, by his lights—to the end.

CLEOPATRA

Shakespeare's Cleopatra had to be acted by a boy, and this did everything to determine, not his view of the character, but his presenting of it. Think how a modern dramatist, a practical man of the theatre, with an actress for his Cleopatra, would set about the business. He might give us the tragedy of the play's end much as Shakespeare does, no doubt—if he could; but can we conceive him leaving Cleopatra without one single scene in which to show the sensual charm which drew Antony to her, and back to her, which is the tragedy's very fount? Yet this is what Shakespeare does, and with excellent reason: a boy could not show it, except objectionably or ridiculously. He does not shirk her sensuality, he stresses it time and again; but he has to find other ways than the one impracticable way of bringing it home to us. What is the best evidence we have (so to speak) of Cleopatra's physical charms? A description of them by Enobarbus— by the misogynist Enobarbus—given us, moreover, when she has been out of our sight for a quarter of an hour or so. Near her or away from her, Antony himself never speaks of them. He may make such a casual joke as

> The beds i' the East are soft.

or reflect in a fateful phrase,

> I will to Egypt. . . .
> I' the East my pleasure lies.

but Shakespeare will not run even so much risk of having a lover's ecstasies discounted. Enobarbus may grumble out gross remarks about her; but Antony's response, as he plans his escape, is

> She is cunning past man's thought.

The lovers are never once alone together; and the only approach to a 'love-scene' comes with our first sight of them, walking in formal procession and reciting antiphonally:

CLEOPATRA. If it be love indeed, tell me how much.
ANTONY.   There's beggary in the love that can be reckoned.
CLEOPATRA. I'll set a bourn how far to be beloved.

ANTONY.   Then must thou needs find out new heaven, new
  earth.

This is convention itself. Antony's

> Here is my space.
> Kingdoms are clay: our dungy earth alike
> Feeds beast as man: the nobleness of life
> Is to do thus; when such a mutual pair
> And such a twain can do't. . . .

is pure rhetoric.[40] And the poetry of

> Now, for the love of Love and her soft hours,
> Let's not confound the time with conference harsh.
> There's not a minute of our lives should stretch
> Without some pleasure now. What sport to-night?
> CLEOPATRA. Hear the ambassadors.
> ANTONY.   Fie, wrangling queen!
> Whom everything becomes, to chide, to laugh,
> To weep; whose every passion fully strives
> To make itself in thee, fair and admired! . . .

is sensuality sublimated indeed.

Not till their passion deepens as tragedy nears does
Shakespeare give it physical expression. Antony leaves
her for battle with 'a soldier's kiss' (it is the first the action
definitely shows) and, returning triumphant, hails her with

> O thou day o' the world,
> Chain mine armed neck: leap thou, attire and all,
> Through proof of harness to my heart, and there
> Ride on the pants triumphing.

A very open and aboveboard embrace. And not till death
is parting them do we reach

> I am dying, Egypt, dying; only
> I here importune death awhile, until

> Of many thousand kisses the poor last
> I lay upon thy lips.

with, for its matching and outdoing, her

> welcome, welcome! die where thou hast lived:
> Quicken with kissing: had my lips that power,
> Thus would I wear them out.

By which time, if dramatist and actors between them have not freed the imaginations of their audience from the theatre's bonds, all three will have been wasting it. Throughout the play Cleopatra herself gives us glimpses enough of her sensual side.

> Thou, eunuch Mardian!
>   What's your highness' pleasure?
> Not now to hear thee sing. I take no pleasure
> In aught an eunuch has: 'tis well for thee
> That, being unseminared, thy freer thoughts
> May not fly forth of Egypt.

But Shakespeare never has her turn it towards a flesh-and-blood Antony, inviting response.

His only choice, then, is to endow her with other charms for conquest: wit, coquetry, perception, subtlety, imagination, inconsequence—and this he does to the full. And had he a veritable Cleopatra to play the part, what other and what better could he do? How does a Cleopatra differ from the common run of wantons but in just such gifts as these? It would take a commonplace dramatist to insist upon the obvious, upon all that age does wither, while custom even sooner stales its infinite monotony!

It is, of course, with his magic of words that Shakespeare weaves Cleopatra's charm. To begin with, we may find ourselves somewhat conscious of the process. Though that first duet between the lovers is with good reason conventional, they seem slightly self-conscious besides; less themselves, at the moment, than advocates for themselves. Not till Cleopatra reappears has this cloud about her vanished; but nothing of the sort ever masks her again.

CLEOPATRA. Saw you my lord?
ENOBARBUS.   No, lady.
CLEOPATRA.   Was he not here?
CHARMIAN. No, madam.
CLEOPATRA. He was disposed to mirth; but on the sudden
  A Roman thought hath struck him. Enobarbus!
ENOBARBUS. Madam.
CLEOPATRA. Seek him and bring him hither. Where's Alexas?
ALEXAS.   Here, at your service. My lord approaches.
CLEOPATRA. We will not look upon him; go with us.

And when she returns:

> See where he is, who's with him, what he does:
> I did not send you: if you find him sad,
> Say I am dancing: if in mirth, report
> That I am sudden sick: quick, and return.

Here is actuality; and forged in words of one syllable, mainly. This is the woman herself, quick, jealous, imperious, mischievous, malicious, flagrant, subtle; but a delicate creature, too, and the light, glib verse seems to set her on tiptoe.

For the scene with Antony, Shakespeare rallies his resources. We have the pouting

> I am sick and sullen.

the plaintive

> Help me away, dear Charmian; I shall fall:
> It cannot be thus long, the sides of nature
> Will not sustain it.

the darting ironic malice of

> I know, by that same eye, there's some good news.
> What says the married woman? You may go. . . .

and pretty pettishness suddenly throbbing into

> Why should I think you can be mine and true,
> Though you in swearing shake the throned gods,
> Who have been false to Fulvia? . . .

Then the vivid simplicities melt into a sheer magic of
the music of words.

> But bid farewell and go: when you sued staying,
> Then was the time for words: no going then;
> Eternity was in our lips and eyes,
> Bliss in our brows' bent; none our parts so poor
> But was a race of heaven. . . .

And so, up the scale and down, she enchants the scene
to its end.

For a moment in the middle of it we see another
Cleopatra, and hear a note struck from nearer the heart
of her. She is shocked by his callously calculated gloss
upon Fulvia's death. Vagaries of passion she can understand, and tricks and lies to favour them. But this
hard-set indifference! She takes it to herself, of course,
and is not too shocked to make capital of it for her
quarrel. But here, amid the lively wrangling, which is
stimulus to their passion, shows a dead spot of incom-
prehension, the true division between them. They stare
for an instant; then cover it, as lovers will. Fulvia's
wrongs make the best of capital; there are poisoned pin-
pricks in them, and the second round of the fight leaves
him helpless—but to turn and throttle her. The rules of
the ring are not for Cleopatra. She takes woman's leave
to play the child, and the great lady's to outdo any

wench in skittishness; she matches vulgar gibing with
dignity and pathos, now loses herself in inarticulate im-
aginings, now is simple and humble and nobly forgiving.
He must leave her; she lets him go. But to the unguessed
riddle that she still is he will return.

Let the actress of today note carefully how the brilliant
effect of this first parade of Cleopatra is gained. There
is no more action in it than the dignity of a procession
provides, and the swifter coming and going and returning which ends in this duel of words danced at arm's
length with her lover. There is no plot to be worked out;
Antony is departing, and he departs, that is all. What
we have is the transposing of a temperament into words;
and it is in the changing rhythm and dissolving colour
of them, quite as much as in the sense, that the woman
is to be found. Neither place nor time is left for the
embroidery of 'business', nor for the overpainting of the
picture by such emotional suggestion as the author of
today legitimately asks of an actress. Anything of that
sort will cloud the scene quite fatally. If the shortcomings
of a boy Cleopatra were plain, we can imagine his
peculiar virtuosity. To the adopted graces of the great
lady he would bring a delicate aloofness, which would
hover, sometimes very happily, upon the edge of the
absurd. With the art of acting still dominantly the art of
speech—to be able to listen undistracted an audience's
chief need—he would not make his mere presence dis-
turbingly felt; above all, he could afford to lose himself
unreservedly—since his native personality must be lost—
in the music of the verse, and to let that speak. So in
this scene must the Cleopatra of today, if *we* are not to
lose far more than we gain by her. There will be the
larger demands on her later, those that Shakespeare's
indwelling demon made on him; he had to risk their
fulfilment then, as now.

But her presenting continues for awhile to be very much of a parade. She is never, we notice, now or later, left to a soliloquy.[41] Parade fits her character (or if Shakespeare fits her character to parade the effect is the same). She is childishly extravagant, ingenuously shameless; nothing exists for her but her desires. She makes slaves of her servants, but she jokes and sports with them, too, and opens her heart to them in anger or in joy; so they adore her. It is not perhaps an exemplary Court, in which the Queen encourages chaff about her paramours, and turns on her lady-in-waiting with

> By Isis, I will give thee bloody teeth,
> If thou with Cæsar paragon again
> My man of men.

but it is at least a lively one, and its expansiveness would be a boon to any dramatist.

She is indeed no sluggardly sensualist; double doses of mandragora would not keep her quiet. What she cannot herself she must do by proxy; she cannot follow Antony, but her messengers gallop after him every post. Her senses stir her to potent imagery:

> O happy horse, to bear the weight of Antony!
> Do bravely, horse! for wot'st thou whom thou movest....

—if perverted a little:

> now I feed myself
> With most delicious poison.

And in that

> Think on me,
> That am with Phœbus' amorous pinches black,
> And wrinkled deep in time.

there is elemental power. And if her praise of Antony for his 'well-divided disposition' seems incongruous; why, a nature so sure of itself can admire the qualities it lacks.

Shakespeare shirks nothing about her. What will be left for us of her womanly charm when we have seen her haling the bringer of the news of Antony's treachery up and down by the hair of his head, and running after him, knife in hand, screaming like a fish-fag? But this also is Cleopatra. He allows her here no moment of dignity, nor of fortitude in grief; only the pathos of

CLEOPATRA. In praising Antony, I have dispraised Cæsar?
CHARMIAN. Many times, madam.
CLEOPATRA.   I am paid for't now.

—which is the pathos of the whipped child, rancorous against its gods, resigned to evil. There is the moment's thought, as she calls the scared messenger back again:

> These hands do lack nobility, that they strike
> A meaner than myself; since I myself
> Have given myself the cause.

And this is a notable touch. It forecasts the Cleopatra of the play's end, who will seek her death after the 'high Roman fashion'; it reveals, not inconsistency, but that antithesis in disposition which must be the making of every human equation. It is the second touch of its sort that Shakespeare gives to his picturing of her; and both, in the acting, must be stamped on our memories.[42]

The end of the scene sees her, with her maids fluttering round her, lapsed into pitifulness, into childish ineptitude. But again, something of spiritual continence sounds in its last note of all, in the

> Pity me, Charmian;
> But do not speak to me.

The complementary scene, in which the unlucky messenger is re-examined, would be more telling if it followed a little closer; but, as we have seen, Shakespeare has hereabouts an overplus of Roman material to deal with. It is pure comedy, and of the best. She is calm again, very collected, making light of her fury; but an echo of it can be heard in that sudden nasty little snarl which ends in a sigh. Charmian and Iras and Alexas have evidently had a trying time with her. They conspire to flatter her back to confidence—and she lets them. The messenger has been well coached too. But the best of the comedy is in Cleopatra's cryptic simplicity. She likes flattery for its own sake. There is a sensuality of the mind that flattery feeds. What does it matter if they lie to her; of what use is the truth? Anger is crippling; but in the glow of their adulation she uncurls and feels her lithe strength return, and this is her only need.

> All may be well enough.

Yet the words savour faintly of weariness too.

Now comes the war and her undoing. Her disillusion first; for Antony, won back, is no longer the all-conquering captain, from whom she may command Herod of Jewry's head—or Cæsar's!—nor does her own reckless generalship prove much help. We do not, as we have noted, see the reuniting of the lovers; we find her at a nagging match with Enobarbus, and turned, with her Antony, to something very like a shrew. And if to the very end she stays for him an unguessed riddle, 'cunning past man's thought', there is much in which Shakespeare is content to leave her so for us—thereby to manifest her the more consummately. By what twists of impulse or of calculation is she moved through the three fateful days of swaying fortune? How ready was she to 'pack cards' with Cæsar? What the final betrayal amounted to, that sent Antony raging after her, Shakespeare, it may be said, could not tell us, because he did not know; and her inarticulate terror at this point may therefore show us his stagecraft at its canniest. But in retrospect all this matters dramatically very little; what does matter is that as we watch her she should defy calculation.

It is futile, we know, to apply the usual moral tests to her, of loyalty, candour, courage. Yet because she shamelessly overacts her repentance for her share in that first defeat it by no means follows that she feels none. She lends an ear to Thidias, and the message to Cæsar sounds flat treason; this is the blackest count against her. But soft speech costs nothing, and perhaps it was Cæsar who was to be tricked. Can we detect, though, a new contempt for Antony as she watches him, his fury glutted by the torment of the wretched envoy? She might respect him more had he flogged her instead! Is there in the sadly smiling

> Not know me yet?

with which she counters his spent reproach, and in her wealth of protest, something of the glib falsity of sated ardours? Next morning she buckles on his armour and bids him goodbye like a happy child; but, his back turned:

> He goes forth gallantly. That he and Cæsar might
> Determine this great war in single fight!
> Then, Antony—! But now—?

It is a chilling postscript.

She is like Antony in this at least—and it erects them both to figures of heroic size—that she has never learned to compromise with life, nor had to reconcile her own nature's extremes. To call her false to this or to that is to set up a standard that could have no value for her.

She is true enough to the self of the moment; and, in the end, tragically true to a self left sublimated by great loss. The passionate woman has a child's desires and a child's fears, an animal's wary distrust; balance of judgment none, one would say. But often, as at this moment, she shows the shrewd scepticism of a child.

From now till we see her in the Monument and Antony is brought to die in her arms, Shakespeare sinks the figure into the main fabric of the play. He makes a moment's clear picture of the welcome to Antony returned from victory. The

Enter Cleopatra, attended.

might be radiance enough; but, for surplus, we have her ecstatic

> Lord of lords!
> O infinite virtue, comest thou smiling from
> The world's great snare uncaught!

When defeat follows quickly, her collapse to terror is left, as we saw, the anatomy of a collapse and no more. Then, from being but a part of the general swift distraction, she emerges in fresh strength to positive significance again; and—this is important—as a tragic figure for the first time.

From wantonness, trickery and folly, Shakespeare means to lift her to a noble end. But, even in doing it, he shirks no jot of the truth about her. She loses none of her pristine quality. If she victimizes the complacent Dolabella with a glance or two, who shall blame her? But how far she would go in wheedling Cæsar—were there a joint to be found in that armour of cold false courtesy—who shall say? She cheats and lies to him as a matter of course, and Seleucus would fare worse with her than did that once unlucky messenger. Misfortune hardly lends her dignity, the correct Cæsar may well think as he leaves her there. He will think otherwise when he sees her again. But it is not till the supreme moment approaches that she can pretend to any calm of courage. She must sting herself to ever fresh desperation by conjured visions of the shame from which only death will set her free; we hear that 'Be noble to myself', 'my noble act', repeated like a charm. Yet she is herself to the end. It is the old wilful childishness, tuned to a tragic key, that sounds for us in

> O Charmian, I will never go from hence.
> CHARMIAN. Be comforted, dear madam.
> CLEOPATRA.   No, I will not:
>   All strange and terrible events are welcome,
>   But comforts we despise. . . .

and in the extravagant magnificence of her grief she is the Eastern queen, who could stir even an Enobarbus to rhapsody, and beggar all description. She has no tears for Antony.[43] The shock of his death strikes her senseless, but her spirit is unquelled. Defiant over his body:

>   It were for me
> To throw my sceptre at the injurious gods;
> To tell them that this world did equal theirs
> Till they had stolen our jewel. . . .

The rest may find relief in grieving; not she!

Shakespeare allows her one touch of his favourite philosophy. She reappears, confirmed in her loss.

> My desolation does begin to make
> A better life. 'Tis paltry to be Cæsar;
> Not being Fortune, he's but Fortune's knave,
> A minister of her will. . . .

This is the note, once struck by Brutus, sustained by Hamlet, of failure's contempt for success. We hear it in life, more commonly, from quite successful men, who also seem to find some needed comfort in the thought. It is a recurring note in all Shakespearean tragedy, this exalting of the solitary dignity of the soul; and he will not end even this most unspiritual of plays without sounding it. He passes soon to a somewhat truer Cleopatra—here is the same thought pursued, though—when she counters Dolabella's bland assurance with

> You laugh when boys or women tell their dreams.
> Is't not your trick? . . .
> I dreamt there was an Emperor Antony.
> O, such another sleep, that I might see
> But such another man!

and utterly bewilders him with the hyperbole that follows, strange contrast to Cæsar's recent decorous regret. But it is on such ridiculous heights that genius—even for wantonness—will lodge its happiness. And the next instant he appears, the manikin Cæsar, who has triumphed over her 'man of men'! She stares, as if incredulous, till Dolabella has to say

> It is the emperor, madam.

Then she mocks their conqueror with her humilities. But the scene is, besides, a ghastly mockery of the Cleopatra that was. Compare it with the one in which she laughed and pouted and turned Antony round her finger. She is a trapped animal now, cringing and whining and cajoling lest the one chink of escape be stopped. There is no cajoling Cæsar. He betters her at that with his

> Feed and sleep:
> Our care and pity is so much upon you,
> That we remain your friend.

Even so might a cannibal ensure the tenderness of his coming meal. She knows; and when he is gone:

> He words me, girls, he words me, that I should not
> Be noble to myself!

One last lashing of her courage; then a flash of glorious, of transcendent vanity—

> Show me, my women, like a queen: go fetch
> My best attires: I am again for Cydnus,
> To meet Mark Antony.

—a last touch of the old frolicsomeness as she jokes with the clown, peeping the while between the fig-leaves in which the aspics lie; and she is ready.

> Give me my robe, put on my crown; I have
> Immortal longings in me: now no more
> The juice of Egypt's grape shall moist this lip.
> Yare, yare, good Iras: quick! Methinks I hear
> Antony call; I see him rouse himself
> To praise my noble act; I hear him mock
> The luck of Cæsar, which the gods give men
> To excuse their after wrath. Husband, I come:
> Now to that name my courage prove my title! . . .

The dull Octavia, with her 'still conclusions', defeated and divorced!

> I am fire and air; my other elements
> I give to baser life. So; have you done?
> Come then, and take the last warmth of my lips.
> Farewell, kind Charmian, Iras, long farewell. . . .

Iras so worships her that she dies of the very grief of the leave-taking.

> Have I the aspic in my lips? Dost fall?
> If thou and nature can so gently part,
> The stroke of death is as a lover's pinch,
> Which hurts and is desired. Dost thou lie still?
> If thus thou vanishest, thou tell'st the world
> It is not worth leave-taking.

Sensuous still, still jealous; her mischievous, magnificent mockery surpassing death itself.

> This proves me base.
> If she first meet the curled Antony,
> He'll make demand of her, and spend that kiss
> Which is my heaven to have. Come, thou mortal wretch,
> With thy sharp teeth this knot intrinsicate
> Of life at once untie; poor venomous fool,
> Be angry and despatch. O, couldst thou speak,
> That I might hear thee call great Cæsar ass
> Unpolicied!

Charmian sees her uplifted, shining:

> O eastern star!

Then follows the consummate

> Peace, peace!
> Dost thou not see my baby at my breast,
> That sucks the nurse asleep?

and in another moment she is dead.

Very well, then, it is not high spiritual tragedy; but is there not something still more fundamental in the pity and terror of it? Round up a beast of prey, and see him die with a natural majesty which shames our civilized contriving. So Cleopatra dies; defiant, noble in her kind, shaming convenient righteousness, a miracle of nature that—here is the tragedy—will not be reconciled to any gospel but its own. She is herself to the very end. Her last breath fails upon the impatient

> What should I stay—?

Her last sensation is the luxury of

> As sweet as balm, as soft as air, as gentle!

And what more luminous summary could there be of such sensual womanhood than the dignity and perverse humour blended in this picture of her yielded to her death—suckling an asp? It defies praise. So, for that matter, does Charmian's

> Now boast thee, death, in thy possession lies
> A lass unparalleled.

—the one word 'lass' restoring to her, even as death restores, some share of innocence and youth.

This scene shows us Shakespeare's artistry in perfection, and all gloss upon it will doubtless seem tiresome. But though the reader be teased a little, it cannot hurt him to realize that this close analysis of every turn in the showing of a character and composing of a scene—and much besides—must go to giving a play the simple due of its acting. As reader he cannot lose by knowing what demands the play's art makes on the actor's. The greater the play, the more manifold the demands! When he sees them fulfilled in the theatre his enjoyment will be doubled. If they are not, he will a little know why, and so much the worse for the actor; but, at long last, so much the better.

OCTAVIA

Octavia speaks a bare thirty lines, and they are distributed, at that, through four scenes. She is meant to be a negative character, set in contrast to Cleopatra; but if only as an instance of what Shakespeare can do by significant 'placing', by help of a descriptive phrase or so, and above all by individualizing her in the music of her verse, she ranks among the play's achievements. She first appears hard upon the famous picturing of Cleopatra in her barge on Cydnus, with this for preface:

> If beauty, wisdom, modesty can settle
> The heart of Antony, Octavia is
> A blessed lottery to him.

—turned, though, to irony by the comment of Enobarbus' grimmest smile and shrug. We then have but a passing sight of her, and only hear her innocently answer Antony's most ambiguous

> The world and my great office will sometimes
> Divide me from your bosom.

with

> All which time
> Before the gods my knee shall bow my prayers
> To them for you.

She departs with her brother; but before the scene ends the ambiguity is resolved. Antony, we learn, will take his first chance to go back to Cleopatra, and Octavia is already befooled. An unpromising beginning for her.

Next we see her parting from her brother, setting out with an already faithless husband, pledge of an amity between the two as hollow to the sound as mocking comment and bland protest can show it; she helpless to make the false thing true. She weeps at the parting. Antony is kindly in deceit—

> The April's in her eyes: it is love's spring.
> And these the showers to bring it on. Be cheerful.

—and, as she turns back to whisper some woman's mis-
givings to Cæsar, he sums up their usage of her, and paints
her quite inimitably in the sense and very music of

> Her tongue will not obey her heart, nor can
> Her heart inform her tongue—the swan's down-feather,
> That stands upon the swell at the full of tide,
> And neither way inclines.

A gentler victim of great policies one could not find.
Another scene shows her shaken off by Antony with the
same kindly deceit, grown colder now; another, her return
to Cæsar, to a welcome humiliating in its sympathy; and
so, impotent in goodness, she vanishes from the play. But
we should remember her, if only by such melodies as

> A more unhappy lady
> If this division chance, ne'er stood between,
> Praying for both parts.

as

> The Jove of power make me most weak, most weak,
> Your reconciler! . . .

The gentle and sustained purity of the cadence is all her
own. To Cleopatra, of course, she is 'dull Octavia', and
Antony, in the fury of defeat, can credit her with re-
vengefully 'prepared nails'; their obvious tribute to a
woman they have wronged.

OCTAVIUS CÆSAR

Cæsar is the predestinate successful man. Beside his
passionate rival, he is passionless; no puritan though. If,
as he says, Antony merely

> filled
> His vacancy with his voluptuousness . . .

it would be his own affair. But how not lose patience with a partner, and such a man as Antony, when he behaves even as boys will,

> who being mature in knowledge,
> Pawn their experience to their present pleasure,
> And so rebel to judgment.

Still, it is his business as politician, to see things as they are, and he knows well enough that his prosaic virtues will never fire the enthusiasms of the Roman mob. He must have the gallant Antony to counter the danger that the gallant Pompey has now become. Not that he under-values himself—far from it! Much as he needs Antony, he makes no concessions to him; insists rather on his own correct conduct:

> You have broken
> The article of your oath; which you shall never
> Have tongue to charge me with.

He must not only be in the right, but keep proving that he is. This alone labels him second-rate.

But is not this the sort of man that Rome now needs to bring the pendulum of conflict to a stand? Such genius as Julius Cæsar's was not to be endured. There was small profit in the zealotries of a Cassius and a Brutus; and to what Antony will bring the Empire we see. Octavius Cæsar may seem no great general. Doubtless at Philippi he 'dealt in lieutenantry'; but at least he does not now send a Ventidius to Parthia to do his work for him, while he is yet so jealous that the work stays half done. And is not the best general the one who does deal in lieuten-antry—when he has chosen his lieutenants well? Here is, at any rate, the industrious, unflagging, cautious man, who wins through in the end, and can say and mean, most luckily for Rome, that

> The time of universal peace is near.
> Prove this a prosperous day, the three-nook'd world
> Shall bear the olive freely.

though, as we saw, the moment's overconfidence in which he says it is followed by a day's defeat. Not even the best-regulated characters can wholly discipline fortune!

Personally he is in many ways, no doubt, an estimable man. If he sells his sister to Antony—and we should not, of course, take a sentimental view of such a marriage—he still holds her dear, and is jealous of her honour. His grief for Antony's death, for his one-time

> mate in empire,
> Friend and companion in the front of war . . .

is not hypocrisy, even though he has, in his own interest, just passed from trying to bribe Cleopatra to have 'the old ruffian's' throat cut to orders that he be 'took alive', to be brought to Rome to walk (as Antony well knows) chained in his conqueror's Triumph. And if he lies to Cleopatra he does but pay her in her own coin. Nor when she outwits him is he angry; he respects her rather.

> Bravest at the last;
> She levelled at our purposes, and, being royal,
> Took her own way. . . .

Not a lovable man, but a very able one; and we see him growing in ability—such ungenerous natures do—as opportunity matures. If he were not rather humourless, we might suspect him of irony in giving as his excuse for getting rid of Lepidus—having had his use of him—that this meekest of incompetent parasites 'was grown too cruel.' And there is a savour of cant, perhaps, in the assurance to poor wronged Octavia that

> the high gods
> To do you justice, make their ministers
> Of us and those that love you.

But one may poke fun at a Lepidus with safety; and righteousness—even self-righteousness—is an asset in public life. In sum, he knows the purblind world for what it is, and that it will be safer in his hands than in a greater man's. And while this is so, does it become us, who compose that world, to criticize him very harshly?

ENOBARBUS[44]

When at last this good friend turns traitor Antony says remorsefully:

> O, my fortunes have
> Corrupted honest men! ...

And Enobarbus himself very early shows a sense of some small part of the corruption:

Mine and most of our fortunes to-night shall be—drunk to bed.

He is the tragedy of cynic mind coupled with soft heart, a tragedy of loyalty to something other than the best one knows.

He is a misogynist confessed, and his talk about women is brutal. Misogyny is recognized armour for a soft-hearted man. But he is as plain-spoken about men, and to their faces besides; nor sparing of himself. Nor is this mere bombast. He sees these chaffering traders in the event as they truly are, and sees further into consequences than do any of them. Antony is his master, and when things go ill he does his best to save him; but good sense and plain speaking will not serve. So far he is a simple variant of the outspoken, honest, disillusioned fellow, a type very useful to the dramatist lacking a chorus; Shakespeare has found it so often enough.

But Enobarbus is not all prose and fault-finding. The rhapsody upon Cleopatra stands out significantly; and when, later, the disintegrating rays of his mind turn inward, they discover him to himself a part and a victim of this timeserving world that he so scorns. It is in the process of his lapse from loyalty, in his sudden collapse from cynicism to pitifulness, that we find Shakespeare's maturer mind and art.[45] We see the moral self-destruction of the man upon whom no man's weakness has imposed, and the completing of a figure of far subtler purport than the conventional, plain blunt image which, at a too careless glance, he may seem to be.

The competent soldier rages against Antony's blundering. But when, with the rest, he could save himself from its consequences, he will not. He chooses the losing side, though his reason 'sits in the wind' against him.

> The loyalty well held to fools does make
> Our faith mere folly. Yet he that can endure
> To follow with allegiance a fall'n lord,
> Does conquer him that did his master conquer,
> And earns a place i' the story.

This is strange doctrine for an admitted cynic. Then he argues back and forth as things go from bad to worse; at last cold reason conquers, and he rats. It is too late now; and he is but half-hearted in treason. We next see him standing silent, aloof, ignored by the sufficient Cæsar—and not sorry to be. Then Antony, by one simple, generous gesture of forgiveness, breaks his heart.

There is excellent irony in his end. That the rough-tongued, thick-skinned Enobarbus, of all men, should expire sentimentally, by moonlight, of a broken heart! But the superficial effect is not all. Thus ends another unbalanced man; and whether the inequity lies between passion and judgment as with Antony, or, more covertly, as with Enobarbus, between the armoured and the secret self, here was tragedy prepared. And we have seen the waste of a man. For this it is to bring sound sense and loyalty into the service of the Antonys of the world. With blind folly to serve, loyalty and good sense must come to odds; then one will oust the other, and master and man and cause go down in disruption.

POMPEY, LEPIDUS AND THE REST

If in a scheme of things so warped by passion, jealousy and self-seeking, the robust Enobarbus is broken, how shall such weaklings as Pompey and Lepidus survive? 'Fool Lepidus' is doomed from the start. He must be everybody's friend; and, while the patching-up of quarrels is in train, who more useful than this mild-mannered little man, with his never-failing, deprecating tact, his perfect politeness?[46] Cæsar condescends to him with scarcely veiled contempt.

> 'tis time we twain
> Did show ourselves i' the field. . . .

But the 'twain' are Antony and Cæsar; Lepidus, the 'poor third' (as Eros calls him later), counts for nothing. The colleagues 'Sir' each other in this scene, we notice, with suspicious courtesy. There is a touch of mockery in Cæsar's. Later, the generous Antony pays him compensation for one quite undeserved snub. The little man has started off the critical debate with Cæsar by a reconciling speech, his only eloquent effort:

> then, noble partners,
> The rather for I earnestly beseech,
> Touch you the sourest points with sweetest terms,
> Nor curstness grow to the matter.

and thereafter is so ready—yet never too ready—with cooing interjections, all ignored. Difficulties resolved, he does mildly assert himself; but Cæsar still ignores him, and is departing. Whereupon Antony:

> Let us, Lepidus,
> Not lack your company.
>   Noble Antony,
> Not sickness should detain me.

The little man is grateful.

He cannot carry his liquor, and they laugh at him for that. And all but the last we hear of him is in the mocking duet between Agrippa and Enobarbus.[47]

AGRIPPA.   'Tis a noble Lepidus.
ENOBARBUS. A very fine one: O, how he loves Cæsar!
AGRIPPA.   Nay, but how dearly he adores Mark Antony!
ENOBARBUS. Cæsar? Why he's the Jupiter of men!
AGRIPPA.   What's Antony? The god of Jupiter.
ENOBARBUS. Spake you of Cæsar? How! the nonpareil!
AGRIPPA.   O Antony! O thou Arabian bird!
ENOBARBUS. Would you praise Cæsar, say 'Cæsar'; go no further.
AGRIPPA.   Indeed, he plied them both with excellent praises.
ENOBARBUS. But he loves Cæsar best: yet he loves Antony:
  Hoo! hearts, tongues, figures, scribes, bards, poets, cannot
  Think, speak, cast, write, sing, number—hoo!—
  His love to Antony. But as for Cæsar;
  Kneel down, kneel down and wonder.

He comes to no heroic end. Cæsar stows him away somewhere, as one puts a pair of old boots in a cupboard.

> the poor third is up, till death enlarge his confine.

It is a sketch of a mere sketch of a man; but done with what skill and economy, and how effectively placed as relief among the positive forces of the action! Shakespeare (as dramatist) had some slight affection for the creature too. For a last speech, when Octavia is tearfully taking leave as she sets forth with her Antony, he gives him the charming

> Let all the number of the stars give light
> To thy fair way.

Should one call Pompey a weakling? He makes a gallant show; but we suspect from the first that facile optimism:

> I shall do well:
> The people love me, and the sea is mine;
> My powers are crescent, and my auguring hope
> Says it will come to the full. . . .

And in a moment we are finding him out. Bad news must be denied; and when it persists, and there is no doubt that the Triumvirs, all three, are to be in the field against him, why,

> let us rear
> The higher our opinion, that our stirring
> Can from the lap of Egypt's widow pluck
> The ne'er lust-wearied Antony.

The scene ends with an empty flourish:

> Be't as our gods will have't! It only stands
> Our lives upon to use our strongest hands.

Pompey is full of flourishes; for he seems to be conscious of a certain intellectual hollowness within him, he whistles to keep his followers' courage up, and his own.

He is a great man's son. He must not forget it, for no one else will, and there is a certain debility in this. He makes peace discreetly, is magniloquent, scores a verbal point or so; no one may say he is overawed. Then comes Menas' offer to cut the throats of his new allies and make him lord of the world; and he answers

> Ah, this thou shouldst have done
> And not have spoke on't. In me 'tis villainy;
> In thee't had been good service. Thou must know
> 'Tis not my profit that does lead mine honour;
> Mine honour, it.

These gallant gentlemen who look to their honour to profit them, and will profit by other men's dishonour! When the Cæsars of the world override them, the world loses little, one must confess. Pompey fades out of the play. To fit him with an appropriate metaphor, he carries too much sail for his keel.

Relays of minor characters, each with a life of its own, help keep the play alive. Shakespeare's fertility in this kind is here at its full; but so forthright is the work that the action is never checked, each character answers its purpose and no more. Nothing very startling about any of them, nothing very memorable as we look back; but this is as it should be, they are accompaniment to the theme, and, at their liveliest, should never distract us from it. Demetrius and Philo, soldiers ingrain, move for a moment in contrast, make their indignant protest against epicene Egypt and Antony in its toils; they have served their purpose, and we see them no more. The Soothsayer does his mumbo-jumbo, a peculiar figure; and Egypt and what it stands for will flash back to us when we see him, in Roman surroundings, again. The messengers are conventional figures merely; but Shakespeare gives to the person of each one the weight that belongs to his errand, and so augments the strength of the scene. Menecrates and Menas come out of Plutarch as famous pirates. Menas sustains the character most colourfully (and his admittance to distinguished company may throw a little light upon the Elizabethan conscience in this matter), but Menecrates is needed to offer a sententious check to Pompey's soaring confidence.

> We, ignorant of ourselves,
> Beg often our own harms, which the wise powers
> Deny us for our good; so find we profit
> By losing of our prayers.

A philosophic pirate, indeed; and we may see, if we will, the more pragmatic Menas, chafing, but scornfully silent in the background.

Agrippa and Mæcenas hover after Cæsar to the end, putting in the tactful word—which ripens to flattery, we notice, the minute he is secure in power. Such men, of such a measure, are always forthcoming. Shakespeare once spices their utility with the humour of their hanging back to hear the latest Egyptian scandal from Enobarbus; they are gleefully shocked by the eight wild boars at a breakfast and the goings-on of that royal wench Cleopatra. Their names apart, there is no history in them, of course. Ventidius, with good dramatic reason, dominates a single scene; and Eros, Thidias, Scarus, Dolabella and the others give vigour and variety to incident upon incident. They and the rest of the incidental characters provide, one might say, a fluid medium of action with which the stronger colours of the play may be mixed.

Of Charmian and Iras there is rather more to be said. They attend upon Cleopatra and she puts them in the shade; but Shakespeare has touched them in with distinct and delicate care. To give them betimes a little importance of their own we have the scene with the Soothsayer with the irony of its prophecy.

> find me to marry with Octavius Cæsar, and companion me with my mistress.

laughs Charmian. And he answers her:

> You shall outlive the lady whom you serve.

So she does, by one minute!

Thereafter the two of them decorate the Egyptian scenes; deft and apt, poised for their mistress' call. Iras is the more fragile, the more placid; Charmian, the 'wild bedfellow', will be the quicker of her tongue, when a word may be slipped in. It is an impudent tongue too; she has no awe of her betters. Worthless little trulls, no doubt! But when disaster comes, and Antony's men, all save one, make their peace with the conqueror, for these two there is no question. They also see what lies behind Cæsar's courtesy; and the timid, silent Iras suddenly breaks silence with

> Finish, good lady; the bright day is done,
> And we are for the dark.

—revealing herself in a dignity of spirit of her own. Another moment and she is trembling again; one would think she could hardly carry her share of the heavy robe and crown. Her service consummated by her mistress' kiss, she dies, as the people of the East can, so they say, by pure denial of life. Charmian, we know, is of fiercer breed. Quick, desperate, agonized, sticking to her task to the end—when all is over she is at it still, fighting her Queen's battles still, mocking the enemy. She laughs in triumph as she too dies.

Notes

1 And a little later he took Coriolanus, another Roman, another man of action, for tragic hero.

2 And we may even read into passages of *Julius Cæsar* a foreshadowing of the breach between the two.

3 The 'strumpet's fool' is some warrant for this; Cæsar's reference to Cleopatra not being 'more womanly than he' is more.

4 There was possibly more matter in the scene at one time. Lamprius, Rannius and Lucillius, whose entrance survives, will hardly have been brought on, this first and last time, for nothing. Was there chaffing between Romans and Egyptians? Nothing is left of it, if so, but Enobarbus'

> Mine, and most of our fortunes to-night shall be—drunk
> to bed.

Or did Shakespeare, having written the stage directions, discover he could make enough effect without them?

5 The Romans had their soothsayers too; but this one, by costume and association, would recall us to Cleopatra's Court. What modern playwright would so opulently employ him—bring him from Egypt, too, even by Plutarch's permission—to such seemingly small purpose? Here we see the extravagant ease of Shakespeare's maturest stagecraft. But the episode yields the exact effect needed, not an iota more.

6 The Folio page displays the relation between the two scenes. But Rowe made an act-division between them, and later editors have copied him (of which more on p. 44, so that even this much of the effect may pass unnoticed.

7 For the further, and important, implication of this, see p. 113 *et seq.*

8 The Folio text itself may have been edited, I know; but not to the measure of another stage than Shakespeare's.

9 I insert 'reliable,' because QI of *Romeo and Juliet* does happen to show some uncertain recognition of scenes.

10 They make their slips, however (see the Preface to *Cymbeline*, p. 58). They followed classic practice, even as today the French, going further, generally begin a fresh scene whenever

a fresh character enters or when a character leaves the stage. Scene does not connote place at all, and the 'scene' of the play, in the pictorial sense of the word, stays unchanged throughout.

11 Strictly speaking, Rowe begins his three days' fighting with Act III, Scene vi, *Actium*.

12 Modern producers, never looking back past them, have, of course, solved the problem with a liberal blue-pencil.

13 This is less true certainly than it would have been twenty years ago, before so many experiments in newfangled (which is really oldfangled) staging had been made. But the normal stage of today is still the realistic stage.

14 This, however (to be accurate oneself), is not our first introduction there. But we only know *where* the Banished Duke should be when we first meet him by a reference to him in the scene before.

15 And if our eyes are distracted by changing scenery the strain will, of course, be worse still.

16 So the Folio calls him, with a variation to 'Thidius'. Theobald, apparently, first made him into Plutarch's 'Thyreus' again, and other editors have followed. But the change is surely too marked for Shakespeare not to have made it purposely.

17 I cannot pretend to say how 'the noise of a sea-fight' was made. Professor Stuart-Jones (who spoke with authority upon one aspect of the matter) suggested to me that what one heard was the breaking of the sweeps of the galleys. But is that—would it have been to Shakespeare's audience—a recognizable sound? I fancy that a hurly-burly flavoured with 'Avasts', 'Belays' and other such sea-phrases from the landman's vocabulary would be a likelier refuge in a difficulty for the prompter and his staff. But there may have been some recognized symbolism of a sea-fight.

18 There is no authority (that I know of) for Scarus' age. But the dramatic value of the contrast between his keen youth and Antony's waning powers is indubitable.

19 Shakespeare elaborates this from a couple of sentences in Plutarch; and the suggestion (from Enobarbus) that Antony almost deliberately 'makes a scene', is all his own.

20 The Folio's stage direction brings Agrippa on alone, but this, his speech pretty clearly shows, must be an error. He may have Dolabella or Mæcenas with him. It will hardly, however, be a symbolic army in full retreat. All the disorder of battle Shakespeare is giving us by sound, its thrills through individuals; and his massed entries are processional. The stage directions hereabouts are all rather cursory.

21 The Folio gives the stage direction

Alarum farre off, as at a sea fight.

in the interval between Cæsar's exit with his army and Antony's entrance with Scarus. This is almost certainly wrong. Antony would not enter upon an alarum with a 'Yet they are not joined.' But it does not as certainly follow that the editors (from 1778 onwards, according to Furness) are right in transferring it to the instant before his re-entrance with 'All is lost.' They may be. But it is an 'alarum afar off', and might come more effectively before, or even during, Scarus' speech. The point is not a very important one. It is hard to tell what sheer dramatic value there was for the Elizabethans in these symbolic alarums and the like, and what variety of effect could be given them. Some without doubt; they speak a language, if a simple one. The effect of that first *noise of a sea-fight* which precipitated Enobarbus' outburst of 'Naught, naught, all naught' is evidently not precisely the same—nor meant to be—as this *alarum afar off* which brings Antony on to the greater crisis of 'All is lost.' We may note that, besides the 'symbolism', Shakespeare gives about a dozen illustrative lines of dialogue to each of the first two battles, to the third about twenty.

22 If we remember his

On:
Things that are past are done with me.

23 Eros is dispatched from the stage for a moment or so by an apparently motiveless 'From me awhile'. The practical need is probably to dispose of Antony's armour; for soon there will be both Antony and the body of Eros himself to be carried off by *four or five of the guard*, Diomedes and (more doubtfully)

Dercetas. But Shakespeare, by merely leaving it unexplained, lets it seem part of the general slack confusion.

24 This is discussed in more detail on p. 75.

25 He made no promise. At most he is so enthralled by her that he would have—feels, perhaps, he must have done. Here is an interesting instance of the way in which Shakespeare makes an *ex post facto* effect, which he knows will pass muster.

26 This, it may be said, was the normal way of employing the inner stage; the action would seldom be wholly confined there. But furniture, and the localization this implies, would tend to focus the action within its bounds. See also the Preface to *Cymbeline*, p. 45 *et seq.*

27 But the stage direction

> *Canidius marcheth with his land army one way over the stage, and Taurus, the lieutenant of Cæsar, the other way: After their going in . . .*

could be more slickly obeyed if there were an inner as well as an outer stage to march over. With two doors only available, it will be a long-drawn-out affair.

28 There seems commonly to have been a trap in the floor of the upper stage. But the use of this and the need to place Antony directly under it would rob the dialogue—would rob the all-important 'I am dying, Egypt, dying'—of much of its effect.

29 Just such a barred gate as shuts in Juliet's tomb.

30 Thus, at least, the (English) Arden edition. But it also presumes (in a footnote) and the Oxford edition definitely states that Cleopatra has so far been upon the upper stage. How and when she gets down is left a mystery.

31 Johnson proposed to insert part of the speech earlier so that the guards could come quietly behind and seize Cleopatra at the cue. But the three previous speeches allow of no such interruption. If Cleopatra had to be *brought* down to the lower stage, it would be ten times worse.

32 There remains the unnatural hiatus between Proculeius' two speeches, if they are both his. Suppose that the upper stage to which Antony is hoisted were not the usual balcony, but

something a little more accessible, to which the guards might climb without delay, and from which Cleopatra might be as easily brought down. The hiatus *may* point to some change in staging, or in the stage itself, or to the shifting of the play from one theatre to another of different resources.

33 This is how Charles Knight tells us they should be dressed (I quote from the quotation in Furness). 'But, he adds, 'for the younger and lighter characters ... some very different habit would be expected by the million, and indeed, desired by the artist.' He is writing in the mid-nineteenth century. The quest for accuracy in these matters is a new thing.

34 We also find Enobarbus entering with a blank verse line. The scene, it is true (see note 4), shows some signs of rewriting.

35 The Folio gives us Antony's entrance before Cleopatra's line

We will not look upon him; go with us.

Modern editions are too apt to place it after, and after her departure, quite obliterating the intended effect. There is even the shadow of a further one. If Enobarbus has already gone to look for Antony, it is with a little train of Egyptians that Cleopatra sails off, leaving the barbarian Romans to their business.

36 *Brutus.* No man bears sorrow better. Portia is dead.
Cassius. Ha! Portia!
Brutus. Dead.

37 Note a technicality. Cleopatra has not to be told that he is going; she guesses or has already heard; she saw him, indeed, confabulating with that fatal messenger. This starts the scene at the needed pitch; no time is wasted working up to it.

38 Enobarbus believes the very worst of her. But, of course, *he* would!

39 Shakespeare finds this in Plutarch, of course; but there it occurs before the last defeat. He adds an ironic value to it by setting it before the intermediate day of victory.

40 The '*embracing*' which Pope and editors after him tagged on to 'thus', is not Shakespeare's direction. Whether he means the two to embrace here may be a moot point; but this sort

of thing was *not* what he meant by suiting the action to the word and the word to the action.

41 Nor is anyone else in the play for more than a few lines; another token of it as drama of action rather than of spiritual conflict. We see in this too how far Shakespeare's stagecraft had outgrown the older, conventional, plot-forwarding use of soliloquies. In his earlier plays of action they abound.

42 The first, her stinging reproach to him for his callousness at Fulvia's death.

43 Throughout the play Cleopatra never weeps. Antony does.

44 Enobarbus, it is worth remarking, is wholly Shakespeare's own, with nothing owed to Plutarch but the incident of the restored treasure and the (altered) name.

45 This minor tragedy is worked out in a few asides. It is done, as it seems, very casually, but it shows what can be done with thrifty skill in the freedom of the Elizabethan stage; divorced from this, it will be ineffective, probably. It is worth remarking that the asides might well, most of them, be joined up into a long soliloquy; and by Shakespeare's earlier method they probably would be. But by parcelling the matter out he preserves the unity and prominence of the main action, and keeps it flowing on. And the whole episode, in its detached quietness, helps to throw Antony's vociferation into high relief.

46 One sees him, for the play's purposes, physically also, as a little man.

47 Shakespeare also throws him into contact with Enobarbus for a brief exchange before the reconciling of Cæsar and Antony begins, and the smoothness and roughness make an illuminating contrast.